Stepping Stones:
The Pilgrims' Own Story

Great hope and inward zeal they had of laying some good foundation . . . for propagating and advancing the gospel of the Kingdom of Christ in these remote parts of the world, yea, though they should be but even as **stepping stones** *unto others for the performance of so great a work.*

William Bradford
Of Plymouth Plantation
Chaper IV

Stepping Stones:

The Pilgrims' Own Story

Compiled and Edited By
Adelia White Notson
  and Robert Carver Notson

Binford & Mort Publishing
Portland, OR 97209

Stepping Stones: The Pilgrims' Own Story

Printed in the United States of America

First Edition 1987

For
Our children
and grandchildren
who are thankful for their Pilgrim Heritage

Contents

Part One: In the Beginning was God — Root and Rise of the Pilgrims

Part Four: A People Capable of Greatness
Some Assesssments and Re–evaluation of the Record

Foreword

A labor of love of many years' duration comes to fruition with the publication of this volume which happily brings together three of the original source documents upon which the history of the Pilgrim Fathers is based: William Bradford's, *Of Plymouth Plantation, Mourt's Relation*, and the Mayflower Compact. In addition, the Notsons have written eight insightful commentaries upon various aspects of the early history of the Pilgrims in Plymouth, giving proper perspective to the place which the Pilgrims occupy in early America. The commentaries deal affirmatively with the Mayflower Compact as the antecedent of the Declaration of Independence and the American Constitution and assemble a wealth of evidence and opinion which support the thesis that the Compact was not only the first written political and social contract in the New World, but also that it served as the inspiration for the American system of democracy based on equality before the law and government by the consent of the governed. Others of the commentaries take a new and deeper look at John Carver, the first governor of the Colony, his important place in the Colony, and his likely connection with *Mourt's Relation*, the *Journal of the Pilgrims*.

As a newspaperman of great experience, as former Executive Editor and Publisher of the Portland *Oregonian*, and as a person who has been deeply interested in the Pilgrim story for many years — he was the keynote speaker at the Triennial Congress of the General Society of Mayflower Descendants in Plymouth in 1978, — Mr. Notson is uniquely qualified to have undertaken with his wife, a former teacher, librarian and researcher, the compilation and editing of this book which contains the important early Pilgrim source documents and thought-provoking commentaries. *Stepping Stones* will be a splendid addition to the library of all who are interested in the history of the early years of America and especially all who are members of the Society of Mayflower Descendants, and their children!

ROBERT L. THOMAS, *Governor General, 1975–1978*
General Society of Mayflower Descendants.

Preface

The bicentennial celebration of the Constitution of the United States which begins in 1987 affords an appropriate interval for some searching study and reassessment of our national life and purposes. Our retrospective goes not merely to the nation's birth but to its beginnings at Plymouth.

The Pilgrim experience stands as one of the most heroic in human annals. The poignant story, detailed in these pages, charts the origin of the great American democratic society. Not only did the Pilgrims struggle successfully against the bitterest of hardships, but they reached for principles that were to survive and become the sinews of a nation.

We invite a thoughtful reading.

Acknowledgements

We gratefully acknowledge our debt to these friends and family for their assistance in producing this volume:

To the late Ernest Richardson, former *Oregonian* artist, for his beautiful concept and authoritative design for the book jacket of *Stepping Stones*; also, for his Declaration of Independence sketch.

To Frank Hockaday, head *Oregonian* artist, for his illustrations so brilliantly conceived and created.

To Dorothy Wood, The *Oregonian*'s long-time executive secretary, for many years of kind and careful clerical help.

To our daughters, Jane Notson Gregg and Ann Notson Poling, for their encouragement.

To the memory of our sister, Elma White Bagg, who told us our story about the Pilgrims was "the most needed book in America today."

To Rosemary Dwyer Frey for recognizing the importance of increasing attention to early American history and giving support to this project.

To Binford & Mort publisher, James T. Gardenier, for his friendly and courteous cooperation and guidance.

Introduction

That our Future will be Worthy of our Past— Objectives and Sources of this Work.

A great deal that one reads and hears about the Pilgrims is likely to be based on misconceptions.

Some of it is fictionalized, and either idealized or romanticized. Much of it is paraphrased and fragmentized. A very large segment is wide of the mark or untrue because of the popular and persistent confusion of the Pilgrims with the Puritans, with whom they shared much in doctrine and from whom they differed importantly.

Early in May, 1970, the British began a five-month celebration of the 350th anniversary of the sailing of the *Mayflower*. Festivities were centered on Plymouth, England, from which the tiny vessel took its final departure September 6, 1620, for the unknowns and trials of the New World.

Dispatches referred to disquieting points raised by several clergymen and "historians" who questioned the wisdom of remembering the Pilgrim Fathers at all.

"They were a miserable lot, thoroughly bigoted, most unpleasant," a local vicar was quoted as saying. "In Massachusetts, they were active in witch-hunting and massacring Indians."

Even the official program of the Mayflower '70 Festivities said:

"They grew rich on the trade in African slaves; they bored the tongue of anyone who denied the Trinity; they hanged adulterers."

The literature does not sustain such summary judgments regarding the Pilgrims. The reports demonstrate a great need for the sponsors, as well as the American people, to re-examine the dramatic and historically significant story of the Plymouth Colony. Noting the 350th Anniversary of the Landing of the Pilgrims, *Time* magazine in its November 30, 1970, issue headlined its write-up as "The Pilgrims: Unshakable Myth" and added: "The year-long celebration is richly deserved, because the Pilgrims were more fascinating in the fact than they ever were in fiction."

Further, this is an especially opportune juncture in our national life for Americans to review our heritage. In 1976 we observed the anniversary of the Declaration of Independence and the nation's birth. At that time we found ourselves with our ideals in crisis, our moral atmosphere polluted. We had grown strong materially, but we had lost our sense of direction and our unity.

Intervening years have brought a geat national revival and a returning sense of optimism and confidence that, from the earliest times, had been the hallmark of American thinking and aspirations. Now we have arrived at the bi-centennial of the Constitution of the United States, that revered document which not only established a new order on this continent, but which has stood as an enduring example of democratic principle to the entire world.

It is appropriate that we should seek to renew ourselves in our spiritual foundations and revive our sense of national greatness and purpose. We need to discover how we got where we are. We need to go back to the Beginnings of America.

Although we have compiled this book for all our people, we are especially hopeful that our youth in these days of trying to find out **who they are** will want to examine their roots by reading this volume of our earliest times.

We have sometimes spoken erroneously of the patriots of the American Revolution as our founders, whereas properly they were the defenders of our democracy and our faith, and not the Founding Fathers. We need to go back 170 years further to discover our spiritual ancestors.

Who, then, were the authors of our heritage? What were the powerful motives that inspired the Pilgrims to sail the Atlantic in a terrifying voyage on the *Mayflower*, and to settle on the bleak shores of New England?

Who wrote, and what were the reasons for establishing, the Mayflower Compact? What new concept did the compact implant in this hemisphere?

How did the Pilgrims differ from the Puritans of the later Massachusetts Bay Colony with whom they are so often confused? What were the relations of the Pilgrims with the Indians and what vital role did this play in their survival? Who was the outstanding personal force in formation of their government and served as first governor of the Plymouth Colony?

What were the vast hardships that the Pilgrims endured and overcame during their first year that led to the celebration of the First Thanksgiving, our oldest American holiday?

The prime objective of this collection of our earliest literature is:

To assemble the essentials of the Pilgrim Fathers' own stories from their journals, papers, and letters and to present them in related order—

To encourage a more general re-reading and re-study of the timeless accounts of bravery, faith and sacrifice—

To reemphasize the spiritual quality of our heritage—

To trace the start of the democratic process on this continent.

We expect to affirm the known and accepted. But, we shall also aim to quiet some of the misconceptions that have arisen through three and a half centuries and to fill in certain vague areas by aligning facts previously overlooked or understated.

Specifically, our main purpose will be to reprint the *Journal of the Pilgrims (Mourt's Relation)* in chronological order along with our abridgement of William Bradford's masterpiece *Of Plymouth Plantation*. Our hope is to integrate these stories and to make them more attractive in style and treatment to the general reader by elimination of tedious and extraneous material.

Our method has been to include all illuminating passages of Bradford's *Of Plymouth Plantation*, from Chapter I – XXI, and omit any needlessly lengthy paragraphs, so that the mainstream of the narrative may be easily followed and enjoyed. The simpler, shorter *Journal of the Pilgrims* is printed substantially in full, with a few clarifying changes. We have also included several pertinent letters and essays in their proper places, such as Robert Cushman's "The Sin and Danger of Self Love" and John Pory's *Lost Description of the Plymouth Colony*.

We have avoided footnotes, by using brackets for explanatory material, and have excluded an appendix by incorporating important material (mostly letters) in the main body of the story. Thus the modern reader who is accustomed to instant electronic knowledge will not have to dig for his facts.

How the Story was Assembled

The edition of the *Journal of the Pilgrims* that first attracted our study was that of George B. Cheever, published in 1848 by John Wiley in New York and London. Cheever had access to the original volume which was written in New England in 1620–21 and printed in England in 1622. We have chosen to follow this edition, although we have studied others which are listed in the bibliography.

We shall start the account with Bradford. At the point of the *Mayflower's* arrival off Cape Cod, we shall substitute the Journal's gripping and detailed story of the first strategic and tragic months in the wilderness for the incomplete rewrite by Bradford in Chapter X *Of Plymouth Plantation*.

The latter's story will then resume, recounting the stern but painfully successful struggles of the colony to survive.

William Bradford began writing in 1630. He laid down his pen in 1650. The manuscript showed liberal evidence of his re-reading because of numerous inserts and marginal notes. As a final act, he compiled his list of *Mayflower* passengers, which numbered 102, including children, and told what had happened to them.

His manuscript contains 270 leaves, with pages 79 to 91 missing. This omission seems to have been an oversight of Bradford's in numbering, rather than any lapse in the record.

Our research of the Bradford story started with the W. T. Davis edition of Bradford's *Of Plymouth Plantation*, published in 1908 by Charles Scribner and Sons.

The Davis text was based on the Commonwealth of Massachusetts edition of 1898 which, in turn, had used the long lost—and at that time newly returned—Bradford manuscript. Recently we have become the proud possessors of the Commonwealth edition which was discovered by a friend in an old newspaper printing plant in Massachusetts. The illuminating decrees, documents, speeches relevant to the return to America of the Bradford papers have added much to our study.

We have spent some time with Samuel Eliot Morison's 1952 edition of Bradford's *Of Plymouth Plantation*. Dr. Morison, late American historian and long-time professor of history at Harvard University, "translated" the original Bradford from the

Commonwealth Edition, converting its archaic forms into modern English.

By permission of Dr. Morison and his publisher, Alfred A. Knopf, we have used his translation as a principal source for our abridgement, for which we express appreciation. For 30 years we have researched Pilgrim literature endeavoring to search out and re-assess facts that might shed further light on the forefathers.

The Bradford manuscript was used before its disappearance, which was during the Revolutionary War, by Nathaniel Morton, William Hubbard, Cotton Mather, Thomas Prince and Governor Thomas Hutchinson, the Tory appointee of the English crown.

All of these writers were vague and sometimes contradictory about certain facts. We believe our studies may help to fill some voids. For instance, many writers leave open to conjecture the identity of the author of the *Journal of the Pilgrims* (*Mourt's Relation*), or follow a presumption that it may have been Bradford.

We believe there is substantial evidence that John Carver, first governor of Plymouth Colony, was author both of the Mayflower Compact and the *Journal of the Pilgrims*. We shall discuss this and other observations in our summary chapters.

Disappearance and Recovery of the Bradford Manuscript

As for the disappearance of the Bradford manuscript, it is presumed that it was taken during the Revolutionary War from the tower library of the Old South Church, Boston. It had been deposited there along with other valuable manuscripts and books by the minister, Reverend Thomas Prince, who wrote his *Chronological History of New England* (Boston 1736) with much use of Bradford.

Prince was something of a collector of historical works. He gave his collection the name "The New England Library". Indications are that he had obtained a continuing loan of the Bradford manuscript from a member of the family and, by consent, had made the library its repository.

When the war was ended, the library was found to be in disarray with valuable books missing including Bradford's manuscript.

Governor Hutchinson was known to have used the manuscript in writing the second volume of his *History of Massachusetts Bay*, published in 1767. Being a Tory sympathizer, he went to England in 1774. Did he take the Bradford manuscript with him?

There were many at the time, and since, who had thought him a logical person to have purloined such a book. He knew where it was and he knew its value.

Dr. Morison feels otherwise. He regards Hutchinson as a man of rectitude, who would have returned the manuscript. He thinks it more likely that a British officer in the garrison that used Old South Meeting House as a riding school during the occupation of Boston simply appropriated this and other books as "loot" or "souvenirs", as military forces are wont to do.

Be that as it may, the priceless manuscript somehow reached the library of the Bishop of London where it was discovered. The library also held other books from the Prince Collection, bearing the labels of the New England Library.

Writings by Samuel Wilberforce, Bishop of Oxford, and Reverend James S.M. Anderson were identified in 1855 as being based on Bradford, and the source, the library in Fulham Palace, residence of the bishop. Charles Deane, for the Massachusetts Historical Society, acted promptly to acquire an accurate longhand transcript, which was published in 1856.

Then began 40 years of diplomatic and legal maneuvering to obtain the original writing, a feat finally accomplished by United States Senator George Hoar of Massachusetts. In the spring of 1897 Ambassador Thomas F. Bayard brought the precious manuscript back to the United States. At a joint convention of the Houses of Massachusetts, held in the Statehouse in Boston, May 26, 1897, the manuscript was placed in the custody of the Governor of Massachusetts.

Senator Hoar delivered a lengthy oration, declaring there had been nothing like the Bradford annals "since the Story of Bethlehem".

In receiving the manuscript from Ambassador Bayard, Governor Roger Wolcott spoke feelingly:

"For countless years to come ... these mute pages shall eloquently speak of high resolve, great suffering and heroic endurance made possible by an absolute faith in the overruling providence of Almighty God."

The Bradford manuscript, after a century plus twenty years, or so, had come back home! It reposes in the Archives Museum of the State House in Boston. We viewed it there, remarkably bright, preserved and protected by a bullet-proof glass, controlled light, heat and moisture—a national treasure!

Adelia White Notson
Robert Carver Notson

Portland, Oregon, 1987

Part One

In the beginning was God — Root and Rise of the Pilgrims

William Bradford,
Of Plymouth Plantation,
Chapters I – XI

They called themselves Pilgrims — *"So they left that goodly and pleasant city which had been their resting place near twelve years; but they knew they were **Pilgrims,** and they looked not much on those things, but lifted up their eyes to the heavens, their dearest country, and quieted their spirits."*

William Bradford, Chapter VII

I   *The Separatist Interpretation of the (Religious) Reformation in England, 1550-1607.*

William Bradford

    I must begin at the very root and rise of the same [and] I shall endeavor to manifest in plain style ... the simple truth in all things.

    ... [It was the desire of the Separatists in leaving the Church of England] that truth prevail and that the churches of God revert to their ancient purity, and recover their primitive order, liberty and beauty.

    ... They laboured to have the right worship of God and discipline of Christ established in [their] church, according to the simplicity of the Gospel, without the mixture of men's inventions; and to have and to be ruled by the laws of God's Word. The other side, though under many colours and pretences, endeavoured to have episcopal dignity with their large power and jurisdiction still retained; with all ... those canons and ceremonies ... and they upheld their antichristian greatness, enabling them with lordly and tyrannous power, to persecute the poor servants of God.

    Contention was so great ... as neither the honor of God nor worthies of the Lord could prevail with those episcopally minded ... They proceeded by all means to disturb the peace of this poor persecuted church ... [yet] it was most needful that the fundamental points of religion be preached in those ignorant and superstitious times ... the more the light of the Gospel grew the more they urged their subscriptions to these corruptions ... They, whose eyes God had not justly blinded, might easily see whereto things tended ... To cast contempt the more upon the sincere servants of God, they opprobriously ... gave unto and imposed upon them the name of Puritans ... And lamentable it is to see the effects which followed.

Religion hath been disgraced, the godly grieved, afflicted, persecuted, and many exiled. Sundry have lost their lives in prisons and other ways: On the other hand sin hath been countenanced ... and atheism increased.

At this day the man or woman that begins to profess religion and to serve God, must resolve himself to sustain mocks and injuries even as though he lived amongst the enemies of religion.

... [Now] by the travail and diligence of some godly and zealous preachers ... in the North parts, many became enlightened by the Word of God, and had their ignorance and sins discovered unto them, and began by His grace to reform their lives ... but the work of God was no sooner manifest in them but presently they were both scoffed and scorned.

... They bore sundry years with much patience ... With heavenly zeal for His truth, they shook off this yoke of antichristian bondage, and as the Lord's free people joined themselves into a church estate, in the fellowship of the Gospel, to walk in all His ways ... **And as it cost them something this ensuing history will declare.**

These people became two distinct bodies or churches, and in regard of distance did congregate severally; for they were of sundry towns and villages where Nottinghamshire, Lincolnshire, Yorkshire border nearest together. In one of these churches was Mr. John Smith, a man of able gifts, who was chosen their pastor. But these afterwards, falling into some errors in the Low Countries, buried themselves and their names.

But in this other church (which must be subject of our discourse) besides other worthy men was Mr. Richard Clyfton, a grave and reverend preacher who by his pains and diligence had done good ... and also, that famous and worthy man who afterwards was their pastor many years, John Robinson. [He and Clyfton were Cambridge, Christ College, alumni.] Also Mr. William Brewster, a reverend man, who afterwards was chosen elder of the church and lived with them till old age.

After these [harassments] they could not long continue in any peaceable condition, but would be hunted and presecuted on every side. Seeing themselves thus molested, and that there was no hope of their continuance there, by joint consent they resolved to go into the Low Countries where they heard was freedom of religion of all men.

[*This church of our story had been meeting mostly in the town of Scrooby near the joining borders of Nottinghamshire, Lincolnshire and Yorkshire at a former manor of the bishops which also was a post station along the Great Northern road, a very ancient way, three hundred miles north of London. William Brewster had received the appointment to the office of the "Post" upon his father's death and resided at the manor. Brewster, whose father and grandfather were clergymen, had spent some small time at Cambridge and then went to the Court of Elizabeth and served that religious and godly gentleman, Mr. William Davison, when he was secretary of State. Davison found Brewster so discreet and faithful as he trusted him above all others that were about him. Brewster attended his master also when he was sent into the Low Countries as ambassador for the Queen. Here he received insight into a brave people fighting for national and religious freedom. But the life of the Court was of short duration, and Brewster was hardly 21 years old when he turned away from its attractions and returned to Scrooby. He assumed the duties as assistant of the "post" and besides became industrious in building up rural parishes.*

Two and a half miles north of Scrooby lived a young lad, William Bradford, on his uncle's farm, and soon, eager to indulge his interest in study, he found his way to Brewster. On Sunday mornings, he followed the meadow paths to Scrooby. Bradford found in Brewster not only religious sympathy but also secular instruction.

About the time Bradford was 16, prelatical persecution had become active. Some of the clergymen whom Brewster had procured for neglected parishes were driven from their pulpits, others were harassed and threatened. As Puritans, the Scrooby reformers had been obnoxious to the ruling powers; now they made themselves vastly more so by becoming Separatists. Brewster was early in the movement and with him came his youthful friend Bradford.

John Goodwin, Pilgrim Republic]

After they had continued together about a year, and exercising the worship of God amongst themselves, notwithstanding ... the malice of their adversaries, they, seeing they could no longer continue in that condition, they resolved to get into Holland which was in the year 1607 and 1608.

II *Of their Departure into Holland and the Difficulties they Found and Met.*

William Bradford

Being thus constrained to leave their native soil and country, their lands and livings, all their friends and familiar acquaintances ... and to go into a country they knew not [except] by hearsay, where they must learn a new language and get their living, they knew not how, it was by many thought an adventure almost desperate ... But these things did not dismay them ... for their desires were set on the ways of God and they rested in His Providence.

... A large company of them purposed to get passage at Boston in Lincolnshire and for that end had hired a ship wholly to themselves and made an agreement with the master to be ready at a certain day.

... [He appeared not by day] yet, at length, he came, and took them in the night. However when he had them and their goods aboard he betrayed them ... and there rifled and ransacked them. And they were imprisoned a month.

... The next Spring there was another attempt made, and others followed. In the meantime, they endured misery enough, and thus in the end necessity forced a way for them.

... For by these so public troubles in many eminent places, their cause became famous and occasioned many to look into the same. Their godly carriage and Christian behaviour was such as left a deep impression in the minds of many. And though some few shrunk at these sharp beginnings, yet many more came on with fresh courage.

... And in the end, notwithstanding all these storms of opposition, they all got over at length, some at one time and some at another, and some in one place and some in another, and met together again, according to their desires, with no small rejoicing. [About 125 members of the Scrooby congregation went to Amsterdam, including the two ministers Clyfton and Robinson, also William Brewster and Bradford.]

III   Of their Settling in Holland and their Manner of Living ... there

William Bradford

Being now in the Low Countries, they saw many goodly and fortified cities, strongly walled and guarded with troops of armed men and beheld the different manners and customs, all so far differing from that of their plain country villages as it seemed they were come into a new world. But these were not things ... that long took up their thoughts, for they had other work in hand and another kind of war to wage. For although they saw beautiful cities ... flowing with abundance of wealth, yet it was not long before they saw the grim face of poverty coming upon them like an armed man with whom they must buckle and encounter. But they were armed with faith and patience, and though they sometimes failed, yet by God's assistance they prevailed.

Now when Mr. Robinson, Mr. Brewster and other principal members were come over - for they were of the last and stayed to help the weakest over before them - such things were thought on as were necessary for their settling and best ordering of the church affairs.

And when they had lived at Amsterdam about a year, Mr. Robinson, their pastor, **and some others of best discerning,** [including Mr. John Carver, a merchant of Essex then in business in Holland, who joined them in Amsterdam. He became a great aid to the Pilgrims and afterwards their trusted leader.] Seeing how Mr. John Smith and his company had already fallen into contention with the church that was there before them, and no means they could use would do any good to cure the same ... they thought it was best to remove before they were anyway engaged with the same [situation].

For these and some other reasons, they removed to Leyden, a fair and beautiful city and of a sweet situation, but made famous by the university wherewith it is adorned.

But being now here pitched, they fell to such trades and employments as they best could, valuing peace and their spiritual comfort above any other riches whatsoever. And, at length, they came to raise a competent and comfortable living but with hard and continual labor.

[*At that time 86 of 131 English were Pilgrims. 57 occupations were represented, most of them having something to do with cloth making, Bradford is described as fustian maker. Brewster and Winslow ran a printing press.*

Henry Martyn Dexter,
England and Holland of the Pilgrims]

Being thus settled, they continued many years in a comfortable condition, enjoying much sweet and delightful society and spiritual comfort in the ways of God under the able ministry and prudent government of Mr. John Robinson and Mr. William Brewster, who was an assistant unto him in the place of Elder. They lived together in peace and love and holiness, and many came unto them from diverse parts of England so as they grew a great congregation.

Such was the true piety, the humble zeal and fervent love of this people towards God and His ways and the singleheartedness and sincere affection one towards another, that they came as near the primitive pattern of the first churches as any other church of these later times have done.

... They had a good acceptation where they lived. The Dutch would trust them in any reasonable matter when they wanted money, because they found by experience how careful they were to keep their word and saw them so painful and diligent in their callings.

The magistrates of the city gave this commendable testimony of them ... they have lived amongst us now these twelve years, and yet we have never had any suit or accusation come against any of them.

IV   Showing the Reasons and Causes of their Removal

William Bradford

After they had lived in this city about 11 or 12 years, experience having taught them many things, the sagest members began wisely to foresee the future and to think of timely remedy. They began to incline to this conclusion of removal to some other place. Not out of any new fangledness ... but for sundry, weighty and solid reasons.

Many that came to them and many more that desired to be with them, could not endure that great labor and hard fare. For though they desired to enjoy the ordinances of God in their purity and liberty of the Gospel with them, yet they admitted of bondage with danger of conscience rather that endure these hardships. Yea, some perferred and chose prisons in England rather than this liberty in Holland. But it was thought that if a better and easier place of living could be had, it would draw many, and take away these discouragements. [Handicrafts were the only occupation open to the English immigrants so the standard of living was low.]

Lastly (and which was not least) a great hope and inward zeal they had of laying some good foundation or at least to make some way, thereunto, for the propagating and advancing of the gospel of the Kingdom of Christ in these remote parts of the world. Yea, though they should be but even as **stepping stones** unto others for the performance of so great a work.

The place they had thoughts on was some of those vast unpeopled countries of America, which are fruitful and fit for habitation, being devoid of all civil inhabitants, where there are only savage and brutish men which range up and down.

... Some from their reasons and hopes, labored to stir up and encourage the rest to undertake and prosecute the same, others again out of fears objected against it, and sought to divert from it, alleging many things, and neither unreasonable nor unprobable ... [to] subject to many inconceivable perils and dangers; as besides the casualties of the sea; the length of voyage was such as weak bodies of women and other persons worn out with age and travail could never be able to endure.

... It was answered that all great and honorable actions are accompanied with great difficulties and must be both enterprised and overcome with answerable courages. It was granted the dangers were great but not desperate. The difficulties were many but not invincible. Sundry of the things feared might never befall; others by provident means might in great measure be prevented; and all of them through the help of God by fortitude and patience [could] be borne or overcome.

V   *Showing What Means they used for Preparation to this Weighty Voyage*

William Bradford

After their humble prayers unto God for His direction and assistance, and a general conference held hereabout, they consulted what particular place to pitch upon and prepare for. Some had thoughts for Guiana; others were for some parts of Virginia where the English had already made entrance and beginning. Those for Guiana alleged the the country was rich, fruitful and blessed with a perpetual Spring where vigorous nature brought forth all things in abundance. So it must needs make the inhabitants rich, seeing less provisions of clothing.

... Yet it would not be so fit for them ... such hot countries are subject to grievous disease and would not so well agree with our English bodies.

... For Virginia it was objected that if they lived among the English which were there planted, or so near them as to be under their government, they should be troubled and persecuted for the cause of religion, as if they lived in England.

... The conclusion was to live as a distinct body by themselves under the general government of Virginia, and to sue His Majesty ... to grant them freedom of religion.

Whereupon two were chosen - John Carver and Robert Cushman - and sent to England to solicit this matter, who found the Virginia Company very desirable to have them go thither, and willing to grant them a patent with as ample privileges as they could grant to any, and to give them the best furtherance they could.

Some of the chief of the company doubted [they would be

able] to obtain their suit of the King for liberty in religion, and to have it confirmed under the King's broad seal, according to their desires.

It proved a harder piece of work than they took it for; for though many means were used to bring it about, yet it could not be effected. For there were many of good worth who labored with the King to obtain it [including Sir Robert Naunton who was Secretary of State under James I and a Puritan sympathizer] ... Some others wrought with the Archbishop [George Abbott] to give way, but it proved in vain.

Yet, thus far they prevailed in sounding His Majesty's Mind ... that he would not molest them, provided they carried themselves peaceably. But to allow them ... by his public authority, under his seal, they found it would not be. Yet, they persuaded them to go on for they presumed they should not be troubled.

... With this answer the messengers returned [to the Leyden congregation] and signified what diligence had been used and to what issue things were come. Many were afraid that if·they should unsettle themselves and go on these hopes, it might prove dangerous and but a sandy foundation ... They must rest, herein, on God's providence as they had done in other things.

[A letter from Sir Edwin Sandys, treasurer of the Virginia Company and also a Puritan sympathizer, gives light on the proceedings:

The agents of your congregation John Carver and Robert Cushman have carried themselves with good discretion as is both to their own credit and credit from whence they came.

And to Sir Sandys their answer: *Now we persuade ourselves, Right Worshipful, that we need not provoke your godly and loving mind to any more tender care of us.*

We are all weaned from the delicate milk of our Mother Country and inured to the difficulties of a strange and hard land.

We are knit together as a body in a most strict and sacred bond and covenant of the Lord, of the violation whereof we make great conscience.

The people are as industrious and frugal as any company of people in the world.

Lastly, it is not with us as with other men whom small things can discourage or small discontentments cause to wish them at home again.

We have set down our requests in writing and have sent the

same to the Council by our agent and a deacon of our church, John Carver,
unto whom we have also requested a gentleman of our company to adjoin
himself (Robert Cushman).] [This statement establishes Carver as the principal agent in "prosecuting of the business".]

 ... At last they had a patent granted them and confirmed under
the Company's seal. But God so disposed they never made use of
this Patent which had cost them so much labor and charge.

 ... This Patent being sent over to them to view and consider,
and also [other] propositions [as to] such merchants and friends who
should go or adventure with them, and especially, those on whom
they [should] chiefly depend for shipping and means, whose prof-
fers had been large, they were requested to fit themselves with all
speed.

VI Concerning the Agreements and Articles between the Pilgrims and such Merchants and others as Adventured Moneys

William Bradford

The Pilgrims had a solemn meeting and a day of humiliation to seek the Lord for His direction; and their pastor took this text from I Samuel XXIII: 3, 4:

... "Then David asked counsel of the Lord again", from which text he taught many things very aptly, and befitting their present occasion and condition, strengthening them against their fears and perplexities and encouraging them in their resolution.

After which they concluded both what number and what persons would prepare themselves to go first; for all that were willing to have gone could not get ready [because of] their other affairs in so short a time; neither, if all could have been ready [were there] means to have transported them all together. Those that stayed, being the greater number, required the pastor to stay with them.

... The others then desired the elder Mr. William Brewster to go with them which was also condescended unto.

It was also agreed on by mutual consent and covenant that those that went should be an absolute church of themselves, as well as those who stayed.

... With this proviso ... [that] any of the rest who came over to them, or [any of] the others who returned ... should be reputed as members without any further ... testimonial.

... [At the time] they were perplexed with the proceedings of the Virginia Company and were making inquiry about hiring and buying of shipping.

Also, about this time, one Mr. Thomas Weston came to Leyden

having much conference with [Pastor] Robinson and others of the chief of them, [including Mr. John Carver] and persuaded them to go on [and not] to meddle with the Dutch or too much depend on the Virginia Company. For if [the latter] failed, he and such merchants as were his friends, together with their own means would set them forth; and they should make ready and neither fear want of shipping nor money; for what they wanted would be provided.

Not so much for himself as for the satisfying of such friends as he should procure to adventure in this business, they were to draw such articles of agreement and make such propositions as might the better induce his friends to venture. [Thus] articles were drawn and agreed unto, and were shown to Weston and approved by him.

And afterwards their messenger, Mr. John Carver, who was sent into England together with Robert Cushman, were to receive the moneys and make provision both for shipping and other things for the voyage, with this charge, not to exceed their commission but to proceed according to the former **articles.**

... So those prepared themselves with all speed and sold off their estates and [such as were able] put their moneys into common stock which was disposed for the making of general provisions.

About this time, also, they had heard, both by Mr. Weston and others, that sundry Honourable Lords had obtained a large grant from the King for the more northerly parts of that country, derived out of the Virginia patent and wholly secluded from their government, and to be called by another name viz, New England. Unto which Mr. Weston and the chief of them [Mr. Carver] began to incline it was best for them to go, as for other reasons. So chiefly for the hope of present profit to be made by fishing that was to be found in that country.

But, as in all business, the acting part is most difficult, especially where the work of many agents must concur. So it was found in this. For some of those in England that should have gone fell off and would not go; other merchants and friends that had offered to adventure their moneys withdrew and pretended many excuses; some disliking they went not to Guiana; others again would adventure nothing except they went to Virginia. Some again [and those most relied on] fell in utter dislike with Virginia and would do nothing if they went thither. In the midst of these distractions, they of Leyden who had put off their estates and laid out their moneys were brought into a great strait fearing what issue things would come to. But at length the Generality was swayed to the latter opinion.

Now another difficulty arose, for Mr. Weston and some other that were for this course, either for their better advantage or for the drawing on of others as they pretended, would have some of those conditions altered that were first agreed on at Leyden. To which the two agents sent from Leyden, Mr. Carver and Mr. Cushman, or at least one of them who is most charged with it [Mr. Cushman] did consent, seeing else that all was likely to be dashed and the opportunity lost and they which put off their estates and paid in their moneys were in hazard to be undone. They presumed to conclude with the merchants on those terms, in some things contrary to their order and commission and without giving them notice of the same. Yea, it was concealed lest it should make any further delay. Which was the cause afterward of much trouble and contention.

It will be meet I here insert these conditions which are as followeth:

Anno: 1620 July 1

1. The Adventurers and Planters do agree that every person that goeth being aged 16 years and upward, be rated at L10 and L10 to be accounted a single share.

2. That he that goeth in person and furnisheth himself with L10 either in money or other provisions, be accounted as having L20 in stock and in the division shall receive a double share.

3. The persons transported and the Adventurers shall continue their joint stock and partnership together, the space of seven years, except some unexpected impediment do cause the whole company to agree otherwise, during which time all profits and benefits that are got by trade, traffic, trucking, working, fishing or any other means of any persons remain still in the common stock until the division.

4. That at their coming there, they choose out such a number of fit persons as may furnish their ships and boats for fishing upon the sea, employing the rest in their several faculties upon the land, as building houses, tilling and planting the ground, and making such commodities as shall be most useful for the colony.

5. That at the end of the seven years the capital and profits, viz. the houses, lands, goods and chattels be equally divided betwixt the Adventurers and Planters; which done every man shall be free from other of them of any debt or detriment concerning this adventure.

6. Whosoever cometh to the colony hereafter, or putteth any into the stock, shall at the end of the seven years be allowed proportionately to the time of his so doing.

7. He that shall carry his wife and children, or servants, shall be allowed for every person now aged 16 years and upward a single share in the division, or if he provide them necessaries a double share, or if they be between 10 years old and 16, then two of them to be reckoned for a person in transportation and division.

8. That such children as now go, and are under the age of 10 years, have no other share in the division but 50 acres of unmanured land.

9. That such persons that die before the seven years period be expired, their executors to have their part or share at the division, proportionately to the time of their life in the colony.

10. That all such persons as are of this colony are to have their meat, drink, apparel and all provisions out of the common stock and goods of the said colony.

The chief and principal differences between these and the former conditions [which were agreed to at Leyden] stood in those two points that the houses and lands improved, especially gardens and home lots should remain wholly undivided to the planters at the seven year's end. Secondly, that they should have had two days in a week for their own private employment, for the more comfort of themselves and their families, especially such as had families.

Because letters are by some wise men counted the best parts of histories, I shall show their grievances, hereabout, by their own letters in which the passages of things will be more truly discerned.

In a letter to John Carver, Reverend John Robinson writes:

About the conditions you have our reasons for our judgements of what is agreed. And this specially, should be borne in minds that the greatest part of the colony is likely to be employed constantly, not upon dressing their particular land and building houses but upon fishing, trading etc.

So as the land and house will be but a trifle for advantage to the Adven-
turers and yet the division of it a great discouragement to the Planters,
who would with singular care make it comfortable with borrowed hours
from their sleep. The same consideration of common employment constant-
ly by the most is a good reason not to have the two days in a week denied
the few planters for private use, which yet is subordinate to the common good.

Send me word what persons are to go, who of useful faculties
and how many ... I am sorry you have not been in London all this while
but the provisions could not want you at Southampton.

There fell out differences among those three that received
the moneys and made the provisions in England; for besides these
two formerly mentioned sent from Leyden for this end viz, Mr. Carver
and Mr. Cushman there was one chosen in England to be joined
to them to make the provisons for the voyage. His name was Mr.
Martin, [Christopher] who came from Essex from which parts came
sundry others to go with them, as also from other places. And
therefore, it was thought meet and convenient that these **Strangers**
that were to go with them would appoint one thus to be joined with
them, not so much for any great need of their help as to avoid all
suspicion of jealousy of any partiality. And indeed, their care for giving
offence, both in this and other things afterwards turned [out to] be
a great inconvenience unto them as in the sequel will appear, but
it showed the Pilgrims equal and honest minds.

To his Loving Friend John Carver, Robert Cushman writes:

Mr. Weston says we take a heady course and is offended that
our provisions are made so far off; as also he was not made acquainted with
our quantity of things ...

You wrote to Mr. Martin to prevent the making of the provisions
in Kent which he did (regardless) and set down his resolution, how much
he would have of everything without respect to any counsel or exception.
Surely, he that is in a society and yet regards not counsel may better be
a King than a consort.

Yet your money which you there must have, we will get provided
for you instantly [It is apparent that the distance of transporting provisions
from Kent to Southampton and the expense was Carver's reason for not want-
ing the purchase of supplies at Kent by Martin]. L500 you say will serve;
for the rest which here and in Holland is to be used, we may go scratch for it.

Thus, their children may see with what difficulties their fathers wrestled ... in their first beginnings ... yet, God brought them along notwithstanding all their weaknesses and infirmities.

[Several of the Leyden congregation wrote of their perplexities in hiring a ship to transport them to Southampton and of other matters.]

Mr. Robinson to John Carver writes:

... The estate of things here is very pitiful (for) want of shipping. ... Divers who are to pay their moneys are behind and refuse to do it until they see shipping provided.

... We depended on Mr. Weston to procure such means for this common business ... that he should not have shipping ready before this time ... cannot in my conscience be excused.

... I have heard that when moved in the business he hath put it off from himself and would come to George Morton [who became Bradford's brother-in-law] and enquire news of him about things as if he had scarce been some accessory unto it.

... Mr. Weston makes himself merry with our endeavors about buying a ship but we have done nothing in this but with good reasons; the one that we employed, Robert Cushman, who though a good man yet is most unfit to deal for other men because of too great indifferency for any conditions.

We have relied upon generalities without seeing the particular course and means for so weighty an affair set down to us.

About the conditions, several from Leyden including William Bradford and Samuel Fuller wrote to John Carver and Robert Cushman:

Many would have been ready to faint and go back in respect to the new conditions ... whereas, Mr. Cushman desired reasons for our dislike ... So we refer him to our pastor's former reasons.

But our desires are that you will not entangle yourselves and us in any such unreasonable courses *as those, viz, that the merchants should have half of the men's houses and lands at the dividend and that persons should be deprived of the two days a week agreed upon for their own particular.*

But requiring you not to exceed the bounds of your commission *which was to proceed upon the conditions agreed upon and expressed in writing (at your going over about it).*

Salute, Mr. Weston, from us in whom we hope, we are not deceived.

... Thus beseeching the Almighty ... as we may with comfort behold the hand of our God for good towards us in this business, which we undertake ... in His name.

Your purplexed yet hopeful Brethren

June 10, 1620

Also, a letter of Robert Cushman's to them:

Brethren:

I understand by letters that have come that there are great discontents and dislikes of my proceedings.

First, for your dislike of the alteration of one clause in the conditions ... there can be no blame on me for the articles first brought over by John Carver were never seen by any of the Adventurers except Mr. Weston [which is possible but unlikely because of the statement that follows].

Neither did any of them like them because of that clause, nor did Mr. Weston himself ... [for] without the alteration of that clause, we could neither have means to get thither nor supply whereby to subsist, when we were there.

Yet not withstanding all these reasons ... here cometh many complaints of Lording it over my brethren and making conditions fitter for thieves and bondslaves than honest men.

And in another letter of his of June 11, 1620:

Salutations:

The many discouragements I find here, had made me to say I would give up my accounts to John Carver, and at his coming acquaint him fully with all courses and so leave it quite.

... But gathering myself I decided to make one trial more.

So advising together, we resolved to hire a ship, about 60 tons [the Speedwell] ... All I now require is that salt and nets be brought there and for the rest we will provide it [in Holland]. Mr. Reynolds, the master, will tarry and bring the ship to Southampton.

VII Of their Departure from Leyden ... with their Arrival at Southampton where they all met together and took in their Provisions

William Bradford

At length, after much travel and these debates, all things were got ready and provided. The small ship, the Speedwell, was bought and fitted in Holland, which was intended to help transport them [the Leyden group]. Another ship, the Mayflower, 180 tons, was hired in London and all other things gotten in readiness.

So being ready to depart, they had a day of solemn humiliation, their pastor taking their text from Ezra VIII: 21:

... "I proclaimed a fast, that we might humble ourselves before our God, and seek of him a right way for us and for our children, and for all our substance."

And the time being come that they must depart, they were accompanied with most of their brethren out of the city, unto a town sundry miles off called Delfshaven where the ship lay ready to receive them.

So they left that goodly and pleasant city which had been their resting place near twelve years, but **they knew they were Pilgrims** and looked not much on those things, but lifted up their eyes to the heavens, their dearest country, and quieted their spirits.

... The next day, the wind being fair, they went aboard and their friends with them, where truly doleful was the sight of that sad and mournful parting. But the tide, which stays for no man, calling them away that were loath to depart, their reverend pastor [Robinson] falling down on his knees, (and they all with him) with watery cheeks, commended them with most fervent prayers to the Lord and His blessing.

Thus, hoisting sail with a prosperous wind they came in short time to Southampton where they found the bigger ship come from London, lying ready with all the rest of their company. After a joyful welcome and mutual congratulations ... they fell to parley about their business, how to dispatch with the best expedition, also, with their agents about the alteration of the conditions.

Mr. Carver pleaded he was employed here at Hampton and knew not well what the other had done at London; Mr. Cushman answered he had done nothing but what he was urged to, partly by the grounds of equity and more especially by necessity, otherwise all had been dashed and many things undone. In the beginning, he aquainted his fellow agents, herewith, ... and they left it to him to execute, and to receive the money at London and to send it to them at Hampton where they made the provisons. That which he, accordingly did, though it was against his mind and some of the merchants, that they were made [at Southampton].

For giving them notice at Leyden of this change, he [Robert Cushman] could not well [have done] in regard of the shortness of the time. [Also] he knew it would trouble them and hinder the business which was already delayed overlong in regard of the season of the year, which he feared they would find to their cost.

Mr. Weston, likewise, came up from London to see them dispatched and to have the conditions confirmed. But they refused, and answered him that he knew right well that these were not according to the first agreement, neither could they yield to them without the consent of the rest that were behind. And indeed they had special charge when they came away from the chief of those that were behind not to do it [Rev. Robinson].

At which he was much offended and told them that they must look to stand on their own legs. So he returned in displeasure, and this was the first ground of discontent between them.

And, whereas, there was wanted near L100 to clear things at their going away he would not take order to disburse a penny but let them shift as they could. So they were forced to sell off some of their provisions to stop this gap, which was three or four-score firkins of butter which commodity they might best spare.

They, then, writ a letter to the merchants and Adventurers

about the differences concerning the conditions as followeth:

Southampton
August 3, 1620

Beloved Friends:

Sorry we are that there should be occasion of writing at all unto you, partly, because we ever expected to see the most of you here, but especially, because there should any difference at all be conceived between us.

... We think it meet to show you the just cause and reason of our differing from those articles last made by Robert Cushman without our commission or knowledge. And though he might propound good ends to himself, yet it no way justifies his doing it.

Our main difference is in the fifth and ninth articles concerning the dividing or holding of house and lands; the enjoying whereof, some of yourselves well know was one special motive amongst many others to provoke us to go. *This was thought so reasonable that when the greatest of you in adventure (whom we have much cause to respect) when he propounded conditions to us freely of his own accord he set this down for one (this was Weston). A copy whereof we have sent unto you with some additions then added by us, which being liked on both sides, and a day set for the payment of money, those of Holland paid in theirs.*

After that Robert Cushman, Mr. Pierce and Mr. Martin brought them into a better form and wrote them in a book now extant; and upon Roberts' showing them and delivering Mr. Mullins a copy thereof under his hand, he paid in his money. And we of Holland had never seen the other before coming to Hampton but only as one got for himself a private copy. Upon sight, whereof, we manifested utter dislike, but we had put off our estates and were ready to come and therefore, it was too late to reject the voyage.

Judge, therefore, we beseech you, indifferently of things, and if a fault have been committed lay it where it is, and not upon us who have more cause to stand for the one [John Carver] than you have for the other.

We never gave Robert Cushman commission to make any one article for us, but only sent him to receive moneys upon articles before agreed on and to further the provisions till John Carver came and to assist him in it.

Yet, since you conceive yourselves wronged as well as we, we thought it meet to add a branch to the end of the 9th article as will almost heal the wound of itself:

But that it may appear to all men that we are not lovers of ourselves only but desire also, the good and enriching of our friends who have adventured moneys with our persons, we have added our last article to the rest promising you again by letter in behalf of the whole company that if large profits should not arise within seven years, that we will continue together longer if the Lord give a blessing.

*We are in such a strait at present as we are forced to sell away L60 worth of our provisions to clear the haven, and withal to put ourselves upon great extremities, scarce having any butter, no oil, not a sole to mend a shoe, nor every man a sword to his side, wanting many muskets, much armour, etc. **Yet, we are willing to expose ourselves to such eminent dangers as are like to ensue, and to trust to the good providence of God, rather than His name and truth should be evil spoken of for us.***

It was subscribed with the names of the company.

At their parting Mr. Robinson wrote a letter to the whole company; which though it hath already been printed [*Journal of the Pilgrims*, London, 1622 - called *Mourt's Relation*] yet I thought good here, likewise, to insert it. As also a brief letter to Mr. Carver.

All things being now ready and every business dispatched the company was called together and this letter read amongst them, which had good acceptation with all and after fruit with many:

Loving and Christian friends,

... Your intended course of civil community will minister continual occasion of offense and will be as fuel for that fire except you diligently quench it with brotherly forbearance.

*... There is carefully to be provided for, to wit, that **with your common employments you join common affections truly bent upon the general good**, avoiding as a deadly plague of your both common and special comfort, all retiredness of mind for proper advantage, and all singularly affected manner of way. Let every man repress in himself and the whole body in each person as so many rebels against the common good, of all private respects of men's selves, not sorting with the general conveniency. And as men are careful not to have a new house shaken with any violence before it be well settled and parts firmly knit, so be you, I beseech you much more careful that the house of God, which you are and are to be, be not shaken with unnecessary novelties or other oppositions at first settling thereof.*

*Whereas you are become a body politic, using among yourselves civil government and are not furnished with any persons of special eminence above the rest [that is, by the crown] to be chosen by you into office of government; **let your wisdom and godliness appear, not only in choosing such persons as do entirely love, and will promote the common good**, not being* *like the foolish multitude who more honour the gay coat than either the virtuous mind of man or glorious ordinance of the Lord.* **But you know better things, and that the image of the Lord's power and authority which the magistrate beareth is honourable** [this paragraph doubtless inspired the drafting of the **Mayflower Compact**].

And this duty you both may the more willingly and ought the more conscionably to perform because you are at least for the present, **to have only them for your ordinary governors which yourselves shall make choice of for that work.**

And to John Carver Reverend Robinson wrote this Farewell letter,

July 27, 1620:

My Dear Brother,

I received enclosed in your last letter **the note of information which I shall carefully keep and make use of, as there shall be occasion.** *I have a true feeling of your perplexity of mind and toil of body, but I hope that you who have always been able so plentifully to administer comfort unto others in their trials are so well furnished for yourself as that far greater difficulties than you have yet undergone (though I conceive them to have been great enough) cannot oppress you; though they press you, as the Apostle speaks ... And the better much when you shall enjoy the presence and help of* **so many godly and wise brethren ... who also will not admit into their hearts the least thought of suspicion of any the least negligence to have been in you,** *whatsoever they think in others.*

Now what shall I say unto you and your good wife my loving sister (Catherine)? Even only this; I desire and always shall unto you from the Lord, as unto my own soul.

And the Lord in whom you trust and whom you serve ever in this business guide you with His hand.

[Following the reading of the letters]:

Then they ordered and distributed their company for either ship, as they conceived for the best; and chose a Governor and two or three assistants for each ship, to order the people by the way and saw to the disposing of their provisions and such like affairs. All of which was not only with the liking of the masters of the ships but according to their desires.

Which being done, they set sail from thence about the 5th of August. But what befell them further upon the coast of England will appear in the next chapter.

[John Carver was chosen governor of the *Mayflower* at the beginning of the crossing at Southampton. Christopher Martin was made governor of the *Speedwell*, assisted by Robert Cushman.]

VIII Of the Troubles that befell them on the Coast and at Sea, being forced after much Trouble to leave one of their Ships and Some of their Company behind them.

William Bradford

Being thus put to sea, they had not gone far but Mr. Reynolds the master of the lesser ship complained that he found his ship so leaky as he durst not put further to sea till she was mended. So the master of the bigger ship (Christopher Jones) being consulted with, they both resolved to put into Dartmouth and have her there searched and mended, which accordingly was done to their great charge and loss of time and a fair wind. She was here thoroughly searched from stem to stern, some leaks were found and mended, and now, it was conceived by the workmen and all that she was sufficient, and they might proceed without either fear or danger. So with good hopes they put to sea again ... not looking for any more lets of this kind; but it fell otherwise.

But after they were gone again above 100 Leagues without the Lands End, holding the company together all this while, the master of the small ship complained his ship was so leaky as he must bear up or sink at sea, for they could scarce free her with much pumping. So they came to consultation again, and resolved both ships to bear up back again, and put into Plymouth, which accordingly was done.

But no special leak could be found, but it was judged to be the general weakness of the ship, and that she would not prove sufficient for the voyage. Upon which it was resolved to dismiss her and part of the company and proceed with the other ship. The which (though it was grievous and caused great discouragement) was put into execution.

So after they had [taken] out such provisions as the other ship could well stow, and concluded what number and what persons to send back, they made another sad parting; the one ship going back to London, and the other was to proceed on her voyage. Those that went back were those for the most part such as were willing so to do, either out of some discontent or fear, they conceived of the ill success of the voyage, seeing so many crosses befall and the year so far spent. But others in regard of their own weakness and charge of young children were thought least useful and most unfit to bear the brunt of this hard adventure.

... And thus, like Gideon's army, this small number was divided as if the Lord by this work of His providence thought these few too many for the great work he had to do.

(The Lord said to Gideon "The people with you are too many for me ... Now therefore, proclaim into the ears of the people saying 'Whoever is fearful and trembling let him return home' ... And Gideon tested them ... "And he of whom I say to you 'This man shall go with you and of whom I say to you' This man shall not go with you, shall not go'").

Afterwards, it was found that the leakiness of the ship was partly [due to] being over-masted and too much pressed for sails. But more especially, by the cunning and deceit of the master and his company who were hired to stay a whole year in the country and now fancying dislike and fearing want of victuals, they plotted this stratagem to free themselves; as afterwards was known and by some of them confessed.

Amongst those that returned was Mr. Cushman and his family whose heart and courage were gone from them before ... as may appear by a passionate letter he writ to a friend in London from Dartmouth whilst the ship lay there a mending. The which, besides, the expressions of his own fears, it shows much of the providence of God working for their good beyond man's expectation. And though (there were) discovered some infirmities in him (as who under temptation is free) yet, after this he continued to be a special instrument of good ...

To his loving friend, Edward Southworth [who died in 1623;

his widow became Bradford's second wife], he wrote the following
from Dartmouth, August 17, 1620:

*My most kind remembrance to you and your wife ... whom in
this world I never look to see again. For besides the eminent dangers of this
voyage, which are no less than deadly, an infirmity of body hath seized me,
which will not in all likelihood leave me till death.*

*We lay at Hampton seven days in fair weather, waiting for her,
and now we lie here waiting for her in as fair a wind as can blow, and so
have done these four days, and are like to lie four more, and by that time
the wind will happily turn as it did at Hampton. Our victuals will be half
eaten up, I think, before we go from the coast of England, and if your voyage
last long, we shall not have a month's victuals when we come in the country.*

*Near L700 hath been bestowed at Hampton, upon what I know
not; Mr. Martin saith he neither can nor will give any account of it, and
if he be called on for accounts, he crieth out of unthankfulness for his pains
and care, that we are suspicious of him. If I speak to him, he flies in my
face as mutinous and saith no complaints shall be heard or received but
by himself. There are others that would lose all they have put in, or make
satisfaction for what they have had, that they might depart; but he will not
hear them nor suffer them to go ashore, lest they should run away.*

*As for Mr. Weston except grace do greatly sway him, he will hate
us ten times more than ever he loved us for not confirming the conditions
... I am sure as they were resolved not to seal those conditions, I was not
so resolute at Hampton to have left the whole business, except they would
seal them.* **Four or five of the chief of them which came from Leyden came
resolved never to go on those conditions.** *And Mr. Martin said he never
received (any) money on those conditions.*

*If ever we make a plantation, God works a miracle, especially,
considering how scant we shall be of victuals and most of all ununited
amongst ourselves ... But God can do much and His will be done.*

*I doubt not but your wisdom will teach you seasonably to utter
things, as hereafter, you will be called to do.*

Your loving friend,
Robert Cushman

These being his conceptions and fears at Dartmouth, they
must needs be much stronger now at Plymouth.

IX *Of their Voyage, and how they passed the Sea; and of their Safe Arrival at Cape Cod*

William Bradford

These troubles being blown over, and now being compact together in one Ship, they put to sea again with a prosperous wind, which continued divers days, which was some encouragement to them; yet according to the usual manner, many were afflicted with sea sickness.

I may not omit here a special work of God's providence. There was a proud and very profane young man, one of the seamen ... who would always be condemning the poor people in their sickness and cursing them daily; and he did not let to tell them that he hoped to help to cast half of them overboard before they came to their journey's end, and if he were by any gently reproved, he would curse and swear most bitterly. But it pleased God before they came half seas over to smite this young man with a grievous disease, of which he died in a desperate manner, and so was himself the first that was thrown overboard ... It was an astonishment to all his fellows for they noted it to be the just hand of God upon him.

After they had enjoyed fair winds and weather for a season, they were encountered many times with cross winds and met with fierce storms with which the ship was shrewdly shaken, and her upper works made very leaky; and one of the main beams in the midships was bowed and cracked which put them in some fear that the ship could not be able to perform the voyage. So some of the chief of the company perceiving the mariners to fear the sufficiency of the ship as it appeared by their mutterings, they entered into serious consultation with the master and other officers of the ship to consider in time the danger, and rather to return than cast themselves into a desperate and inevitable peril. And truly, there was great distraction and difference of opinion amongst the mariners themselves; fain would they do what could be for their wages sake, being now near half over the seas, and on the other hand, they were loath to hazard their lives too desperately. But in examining of all opinions, the master and others affirmed they knew the ship to be strong and firm under water; and for the buckling of the main beam, there was a great iron screw the passengers brought out of Holland, which would raise the beam into place; the which being done, the carpenter and master affirmed that with a post put under it, set firm in the lower deck and otherwise bound, he would make it sufficient. And as for the decks and upper works, they would caulk them as well as they could ... So they committed themselves to the will of God, and resolved to proceed.

In sundry of these storms the winds were so fierce and the seas so high, as they could not bear a knot of sail, but were forced to hull [lay-to under very short sail and drift with the wind] for divers days together. And in one of them, as they lay at hull in a mighty storm, a lusty young man, called John Howland, coming upon some occasion above the gratings was with a seele [roll] thrown into the sea. But it pleased God that he caught hold of the top sail halyards which hung overboard and ran out at length. Yet he held his hold (though he was sundry fathoms under water) till he was hauled up by the same rope to the brim of the water, and then with a broad hook and other means got into the ship again and his life saved. And though he was somewhat ill with it, yet he [became John Carver's aide] and lived many years after and was a profitable member both of the church and commonwealth. In all this voyage there died but one of the passengers which was William Butten, a youth, and servant to Dr. Samuel Fuller, as they drew near the coast.

After long beating at Sea, they fell with that land which is called Cape Cod; the which being made and certainly known to be it, they were not a little joyful.

After some deliberation amongst themselves and with the master of the ship, they tacked about and resolved to stand for the Southward (the wind and weather being fair) to find some place about the Hudson River for their habitation. But, after they had sailed that course about half the day, they fell among dangerous shoals and roaring breakers, and they were so far entangled, therewith, as they conceived themselves in great danger, and the wind shrinking upon them withal, they resolved to bear up again for the Cape and thought themselves happy to get out of those dangers before night overtook them, as by God's providence they did. And the next day they got into the Cape Harbor where they rid in safety.

Being thus in a safe harbor, they fell on their knees and blessed the God of Heaven who had brought them over the vast and furious ocean and delivered them from the perils and miseries thereof, again to set their feet on the firm and stable earth, their proper element.

But here I cannot but stay and make a pause, and stand half amazed at this poor people's present condition ... Being thus passed the vast ocean, and a sea of troubles before in their preparation ... they now had no friends to welcome them nor inns to entertain or refresh their weatherbeaten bodies; no houses or much less towns to repair to, to seek for succour. Savage barbarians, when they met them, were readier to fill their sides full of arrows.

What could now sustain them but the Spirit of God and His grace?

X   *Showing how they sought out a place of Habitation; and what Befell them Thereabout*

William Bradford

[Bradford in this chapter paraphrases the *Journal of the Pilgrims* from November 11 to December 15. He apparently decides not to continue the report given in the daily diary which had already been published when Bradford wrote *Of Plymouth Plantation*.

Journal of the Pilgrims in full follows the next chapter including the Mayflower Compact.

Bradford also changed his method at this point, saying: "The rest of this history, if God give me life and opportunity, I shall, for brevities sake, handle by way of annals." He called it his second book.]

XI   The Remainder of Anno 1620 (The Mayflower Compact)

William Bradford

I shall a little return back and begin with a combination made by them before they came ashore; being the **first foundation of their government in this place**. Occasioned partly by the discontented and mutinous speeches that some of the strangers amongst them had let fall ... in the ship: that when they came ashore they would use their own liberty for none had power to command them, the patent they had being for Virginia and not for New England. Such an act by them done [the Mayflower Compact having been signed], this their condition considered, might be as firm as any patent and in some respects more sure.

After this they chose, or rather confirmed, Mr. John Carver, a man godly and well approved amongst them, their goods or common store (which were long in unloading for want of boats, foulness of the winter weather and the sickness of divers of them) and also began some small cottages for their habitation; as time would admit, they met and consulted laws and orders, both for their civil and military government as the necessity of their condition did require, still adding, thereunto, as urgent occasion in several times and cases did require.

In these hard and difficult beginnings, they found some discontents and murmurings arise amongst some, and mutinous speeches ... in others, but they were soon quelled and overcome by the wisdom, patience, and just and equal carriage of things by the Governor and better part which clave faithfully together in the main.

But that which was most sad and lamentable was that in two

or three months time half their company died, especially in January and February, being the depth of winter, and wanting houses and other comforts. Of 102 persons scarce 50 remained. And of these, in the time of most distress, there were but six or seven sound persons who to their great commendations, be it spoken, spared no pains night or day, but with abundance of toil and hazard of their own health, fetched them wood, made them fires, dressed them meat, made their beds, washed their loathsome clothes, clothed and unclothed them. In a word, did all the homely and necessary offices for them which dainty and queasy stomachs cannot endure to hear named; and all this willingly and cheerfully without any grudging in the least; showing herein, their true love unto their friends and brethren; a rare example and worthy to be remembered.

[The Indian Relations will follow in the *Journal of the Pilgrims*. Bradford also gives the terms of the Treaty of Peace which he says "hath now continued this 24 years" - this indicates date of Bradford's writing this chapter was 1649.]

... The spring now approaching, it pleased God the mortality began to cease among them which put new life into them.

... Many smaller matters I omit, sundry of them having been **already published in a Journal made by one of the company**, and some other passages of journeys and relations already published to which I refer those that are willing to know them more particularly.

Part Two

Truly Bent upon the General Good

Journal of the Pilgrims,
written in America, 1620–21,
published in London, 1622

"... *Having undertaken for the Glory of God, and the Advancement of the Christian Faith ... these presents solemnly and mutually ... combine ourselves together for our better ordering and preservation; ... and by virtue hereof to enact ... such just and equal laws ... thought most meet for the General Good of the Colony*"

Mayflower Compact,
November 11, 1620

"*To each is given the Manifestation of the Spirit for the Common Good*"

I Corinthians 12:7

"... *that with your common employments you join common affections* **Truly Bent upon the General Good**"

Rev. John Robinson in his parting letter to the Pilgrims

Journal of the Pilgrims
or *Mourt's Relation*

Written in Plymouth, New England, 1620–21 – first published in 1622 as *Mourt's Relation* by G. Mourt in England.

Reprinted from the Original Volume in 1848 by George B. Cheever whose Publishers were John Wiley, 161 Broadway, New York, and 13 Pater Noster Row, London

Preface

    G. Mourt is regarded as having been George Morton, brother-in-law of Governor William Bradford, who came to the colony in 1623 but died in June, 1624, a gracious servant of God, unfeigned lover and promoter of the common good, and growth of the plantation, and faithful in whatever public employment he was entrusted with. He came in the Anne about the end of July 1623 and was among the best and most useful members of the body who arrived in that vessel

    ... George Morton seems to have superintended the publication of the Journal, and in consequence the volume has generally gone very inappropriately, by the name of "Mourt's Relation". A more proper title is the "Journal of the Pilgrims"

George B. Cheever

Courteous Reader:

Be entreated to make a favorable construction of my foreward-ness in publishing these ensuing discourses: the desire of carrying the Gospel of Christ into these foreign parts amongst those people that as yet have had no knowledge nor taste of God; as also to procure unto themselves and others a quiet and comfortable habitation.

... it has pleased God even beyond our expectation in so short a time to give hope of letting some of them see (though some he hath taken out of the vale of tears) some grounds of hope of the accomplishment of both these ends ...

And as myself, then, I much desire and shortly hope to effect, if the Lord wills, the putting of my shoulder in this hopeful business and in the meantime, **these relations coming to my hand from my known and faithful friends on whose writings I do much rely, I thought it not amiss to make them more general, hoping of a cheerful proceeding, both of Adventurers and Planters.**

Thy Friend,

G. Mourt
(George Morton)

*Commencing with their departure from Leyden until their arrival in Cape Cod Harbor, the time was **108 days**.*

From **August 5** the date of their first setting sail from Southampton in England to November 10th, the date of anchorage in Cape Cod Harbor 98 days - length of voyage across the Atlantic. But from their last setting sail after being compelled to put back to Plymouth because of the leaking of the *Speedwell* on which day, September 6, *Journal of the Pilgrims commences*, the voyage occupies **66 days** from port to port.

It was a boisterous passage –

G.B.C.

[Note: Although the Journal mentions the departure from Plymouth September 6, 1620, it begins the basic narrative November 9, the day the *Mayflower* reached Cape Cod. As the tiny vessel eased into what is now Provincetown harbor, the Mayflower Compact was composed and signed. John Carver, who had served as "governor" of the *Mayflower* was then confirmed as governor of the colony. The transactions, which set up the first democratic government on the American continent, were completed November 11.]

A *Relation of Journal of the Proceedings of the Plantation settled at Plymouth in New England*

Wednesday, the Sixth of September [1620], the wind coming East North East, [in] a fine small gale, we loosed from Plymouth; having been kindly entertained ... by divers friends there dwelling. After many difficulties in boisterous storms, at length, by God's Providence, upon the 9th of November following, by break of the day, we espied land which we deemed to be Cape Cod, and afterward proved it. And the appearance of it much comforted us: especially seeing so goodly a land, and wooded to the brink of the sea. It caused us to rejoice together, and praise God that had given us once again to see land.

And thus we made our course South Southwest purposing to go to a river [Hudson], ten leagues to the south of the Cape: but, at night, the wind being contrary, we put around again for the Bay of Cape Cod. And upon the 11th of November, we came to an anchor in the Bay: which is a good harbour and a pleasant Bay; circled round, except in the entrance, which is about four miles over from land to land; compassed about to the very sea, with oaks, pines, juniper, sassafras, and other sweet wood. It is a harbour wherein a thousand sail of Ships may safely ride.

There we [replenished] ourselves with wood and water, and refreshed our people; while our Shallop was fitted to coast the Bay, to search for [a place] of habitation.

There was [there] the greatest store of fowl that ever we saw. And, every day, we saw whales playing hard by us. Of which, in that place, if we had [had] instruments and means to take them, we might have made a very rich return in [oil] ... for cod, we assayed; but found none. There is a good store, no doubt, in their season.

Neither got we any fish all the time we lay there, but some few little ones on the shore. We found great mussels, and very fat and full of sea pearls: but we could not eat them, for they made us all sick that did eat, sailors as well as passengers.

... The Bay [Provincetown harbor] is so ... circling that, before we could come to anchor, we went round all the points of the compass. We could not come near the shore, by three-quarters of an English mile, because of shallow water: which was a great prejudice to us. For our people, going on shore, were forced to wade a bowshot or two, in going along; which caused many to get colds and coughs, for it was many times, freezing cold weather.

This day before we came to harbour, observing some not well affected by unity and concord but gave some appearance of faction, it was thought good there should be an association and agreement that we should combine together in one body and to submit to such government and governors as we should by common consent agree to make, and choose, and set our hands to this that follows word for word:

Mayflower Compact:

In the name of God, Amen, we whose names are underwritten, the loyal subjects of our dread sovereign lord, King James, by the grace of God of Gt. Britain, France, Ireland, King Defender of the Faith, etc.

Having undertaken for the glory of God and advancement of the Christian faith, and honor of our King and Country, a voyage to plant the first colony in the Northern parts of Virginia, do by these presents **solemnly and mutually in the presence of God and of one another, covenant, and combine ourselves together into a civil body politic for our better ordering and preservation, and furtherance of the ends aforesaid; and by virtue hereof to enact, constitute, and frame such just and equal laws, ordinances, acts, constitutions, offices from time to time, as shall be thought most meet and convenient for the general good of the colony; unto which we promise all due submission and obedience.**

In witness whereof we have hereunder subscribed our names

at Cape Cod, the 11th of November, in the year of the reign of our
Sovereign Lord King James, of England, France, and Ireland the
eighteenth and of Scotland the fifty-fourth. Anno Domini **1620**

John Carver	John Tilley
William Bradford	Francis Cooke
Edward Winslow	Thomas Rogers
William Brewster	Thomas Tinker
Isaac Allerton	John Rigdale
Myles Standish	Edward Fuller
John Alden	John Turner
Samuel Fuller	Francis Eaton
Christopher Martin	James Chilton
William Mullins	John Crackston
William White	John Billington
Richard Warren	Moses Fletcher
John Howland	John Goodman
Stephen Hopkins	Degory Priest
Edward Tilley	Thomas Williams
Gilbert Winslow	Richard Gardner
Edmond Margeson	John Allerton
Peter Brown	Thomas English
Richard Britteridge	Edward Doty
George Soule	Edward Leister
Richard Clarke	

The same day, November 11, so soon as we could, we set
ashore fifteen or sixteen men, well armed, ... to fetch wood, for we
had none left; and also to see what the land was, and what inhabitants
they could meet with.

They found it to be a small neck of land. On this side where
we lay is the Bay; and on the further side the sea. The ground or
earth [consists of] sandhills, much like the Downes [dunes] in
Holland, but much better. The crust of the earth a spit's depth, excellent black earth: all wooded with oaks, pines, sassafras, juniper,
birch, holly, vines, some ash, walnut. The wood for the most part
open, and without underwood; fit either to go, or ride in.

At night our people returned, but found not any person, nor

habitation, and laded their Boat with juniper, which smelled very sweet and strong, and of which we burned most of the time we lay there.

Monday, the 13th of November, we drew our Shallop on land to mend and repair her, having been forced to cut her down in bestowing her between decks. It took 16 or 17 days before the carpenter finished her. While we thus lay still, hoping our Shallop would be ready in five or six days - our carpenter made slow work of it - so that our people impatient of delay decided for our better furtherance to travel by land into the country, which was not without the appearance of danger, not having the Shallop with them nor means to carry provisions, but on their backs; so that they might see whether it might be fit for us to settle in or no and to observe a river they thought they saw as they sailed into the harbour.

The willingness of the persons was liked, but the thing itself, in regard of the danger was rather permitted than approved, and **so with cautions, directions and instructions, sixteen men were set out with every man his musket, sword, and corslet,** under the conduct of Captain Myles Standish, unto whom was adjoined for counsel and advise, William Bradford, Stephen Hopkins and Edward Tilley.

Our [other] people went on shore to refresh themselves, and our women to wash, as they had great need.

Wednesday, the 15th of November, they were set a shore, and when they had ordered themselves in the order of a single file, and marched about the space of a mile by the sea they espied five or six people, with a dog, coming towards them, who were Savages. When they saw the Pilgrims, they ran into the woods and whistled their dog after them. First, they supposed them to be Master Jones and some of his men, for they were ashore, ... but after they knew them to be Indians, they marched after them into the woods, lest other of the Indians should lie in ambush.

But when the Indians saw our men following, they ran away with might and main ... they continued after them, for it was the way they intended to go, but they could not come near them. They followed them that night ten miles by the trace of their footings; and at a turning perceived how they ran up a hill, to see whether they were being followed.

At length, night came upon them, and they were constrained to take up their lodging so they set forth three sentinels; as for the rest, some kindled a fire, and others fetched wood, and there held our rendezvous that night.

In the morning as soon as we could see the trace, we proceeded on our journey, and had the track until we had compassed the head of a long creek, and there they [the Indians] took into another woods, and we after them, supposing to find some of their dwellings. But we marched through boughs and bushes and under hills and vallies, which tore our very armour in pieces, and yet we could meet with none of them, nor their houses, nor find any fresh water which we greatly desired and stood in need of. We brought neither beer nor water with us, and our victuals were only bisket and Holland cheese, and a little bottle of aquavite, so as we were sore a thirst.

About ten o'clock we came into a deep valley, full of brush ... and long grass, through which we found little paths or tracts. There we saw a deer and found springs of fresh water of which we were heartily glad, and sat down and drank our first New England water with as much delight as ever we drank drink in all our lives.

When we had refreshed ourselves, we directed our course full South, that we might come to the shore, which within a short while after we did, and there made a fire, that they in the Ship might see where we were ... and so marched on towards this supposed river. As we went in another valley, we found a fine clear pond of fresh water, being about a musket shot broad. There grew many small vines and much sassafras; also fowl and deer haunted there. From thence, we went on and found much plain ground, about fifty acres, fit for the plow, and some signs where the Indians had formerly planted their corn.

After this, some thought it best for nearness of the river to go down and travel on the sea sands, by which means, some of our men became tired and lagged behind. So we stayed and gathered them up and struck into the Land again, where we found a little path to certain heaps of sand. One was covered with old mats, and had a wooden thing like a mortar whelmed on the top of it, and an earthen pot layed in a little hole at the end thereof. We musing what it might be, dug and found a bow, and as were thought arrows, but they were rotten. We supposed there were many other things, but because we deemed them graves, we put in the bow again and made it up as it was, and left the rest untouched, because we thought it would be odious unto them to ransack their sepulchers. We went on further and found new stubble, of which they had gotten corn this year and many walnut trees full of nuts, and great store of strawberries, and some vines.

Passing thus a field or two ... we found where a house had been, and four or five old planks laid together. We also found a great kettle, probably a Ship's kettle, brought out of Europe. There was also a heap of sand, made like the former, but it was newly done. We dug this up and in it we found a little old basket full of fair Indian corn, and dug further and found a fine, great, new basket full of very fair corn of this year, with some 36 goodly ears of corn, some yellow, and some red, and others mixed with blue, which was a very goodly sight. The basket was round and narrow at the top and held about three or four bushels, which was as much as two of us could lift up from the ground.

But whilst we were busy about these things, we set our men as sentinels in a round ring - all but two or three which dug up the corn. We were in suspense, what to do with it, and the kettle, and as much of the corn as we could carry away with us. When our Shallop came, if we could find any of the people, and come to parley with them, we would give them the kettle again, and satisfy them for their corn. So we took all the ears and put a good deal of loose corn in the kettle for two men to bring away on a staff. Besides, they that put any into their pockets filled the same. The rest we buried again for we were so laden with armour that we could carry no more.

Not far from this place, we found the remainder of an old Fort or Palizade, which, as we conceived, had been made by some Christians: this was also hard by that place which we thought had been a river, unto which we went and found it so to be. It was divided into two arms by a high bank, standing right by the cut or mouth which came from the Sea; that which was next unto us was the less, the other arm was more than twice as big, and not unlike an harbour for ships; but whether it be a fresh river, or only an indraught of the Sea, we had no time to discover, for we had commandment to be out but two days.

Here also we saw two canoes, the one on the one side, the other on the other side; we could not believe it was a canoe, till we came near it: so we returned leaving the further discovery hereof to our Shallop, and came that night back again to the fresh water pond.

There we made our rendezvous, making a great fire and a Baricado to windward of us. We kept good watch with three Sentinels all night, everyone standing when his turn came, while five or six inches of Match was burning. It proved a rainy night.

In the morning, we took our Kettle and sunk it in the pond, and trimmed our muskets, for few of them would go off because of the wet, and so coasted the wood again, in which we were shrewdly puzzled, and lost our way.

As we wandered, we came to a tree, where a young Spritt was bowed down over a bow, and some acorns strewn underneath. Stephen Hopkins said, it had been to catch some deer, so, as we were looking at it, William Bradford, being in the rear, when he came looked also upon it, and as he went about it, gave a sudden jerk up, and he was immediately caught by the leg. It was a very pretty devise, made with a rope of their own making, and having a noose as artifically made as any roper in England can make, and as like ours as can be, which we brought away with us.

In the end we got out of the wood, and [strayed] about a mile too high above the creek, where we saw three bucks, but we had rather have had one of them. We also did spring three couple of partridges; as we came along by the creek, we saw great flocks of wild geese and ducks, but they were very fearful of us.

So we marched some while in the woods, some while on the sands, and other while in the water up to the Knees, till at length we came near the Ship, and then we, shot off our pieces, and the long boat came to fetch us; Master Jones and Master Carver, with many of our people, came to meet us.

And thus we came both weary and welcome home, and delivered our corn into the store, to be kept for seed, for we knew not how to come by any, and therefore were very glad. **We purposed**

as soon as we could meet with any of the inhabitants of that place to make them large satisfaction. This was our first discovery whilst our Shallop was in repairing.

Our people did make things as fitting as they could, and as time would in seeking out wood, and helving (furnish with a handle) of tools, and sawing of timber to build a new Shallop, but the discommodiousness of the harbour did much hinder us, for we could neither go to, nor come from the shore, but at high water, which was much to our hindrance and hurt, for oftentimes, they waded to the middle of the thigh, and oft to the knees, to go and come from land; Some did it necessarily, and some for their own pleasure, but it brought to the most if not all, coughs and colds, the weather proving suddenly cold and stormy, which afterward turned to the scurvey, whereof many died.

When our Shallop was fit, there were appointed some 24 men of our own and armed to go, and make a more full discovery of the rivers before mentioned. Master Jones was desirous to go with us, and took such of his sailors who would be useful to us. We made Master Jones our leader for we thought it best to gratify his kindness and forwardness. When we were set forth, it proved rough weather and [there were] cross winds so we were constrained, some in the Shallop and others in the long boat to row to the nearest shore, that the wind would suffer them to go into, and wade out above the knees. We marched 6 or 7 miles further, and appointed the shallop to come after us as soon as it could. It blew and did snow all that day and night, and froze withal. Some of our people took the original of their death there. The next day about 11 o'clock, our shallop came to us, and we shipped ourselves to the river we formerly discovered, which we named Cold Harbour; which when we came, we found it not navigable for ships, yet we thought it might be a good harbour for boats for it flows 12 feet at high water. We landed our men between the two creeks, and marched some 4 or 5 miles by the greater of them, and the Shallop followed us; At length night grew on, and our men were tired with marching up and down the steep hills and deep vallies which lay a foot thick with snow. Master Jones was desirous we should take up our lodging, though some would have gone farther; so we made our rendezvous for that night under a few pine trees. As it fell out, we got three fat geese and six ducks for our supper which we ate with soldiers' stomachs, for we had eaten little all that day. Our resolution next morning was to go up to the head of the river for we supposed it would prove fresh water, but in the morning our resolution held not, for many liked not the hilliness of the soil, and badness of the harbor. So we turned towards the other creek that we might go over and look for the rest of the corn we left behind when we were here before. When we came to the creek, we saw the canoe on the dry ground, and a flock of geese on the river at which one made a shot and killed a couple of them. This done the canoe carried us over by seven or eight at once. **Then we marched to the place where we had found the corn formerly which place we called Corn Hill and dug and found the rest, of which we were very glad.** We dug in the place a little further and found a bottle of oil, two or three baskets of Indian wheat, and a bag of beans, with a good many of fair wheat ears. Whilst some of us were digging up this, some others found another heap of corn which they dug up also, so we had in all ten bushels which will serve sufficiently for seed.

And surely it was God's good providence that we found this corn; we had in all likelihood never seen a grain of it, if we had not made our first Journey, for now the ground was covered with snow.

... Master Jones was earnest to go aboard, foul weather being towards, but sundry desired to make further discoveries, and to find out the Indians' habitations. So we sent home with him our weakest people and some that were sick, and all the corn, and **18 of us stayed still, and lodged there that night and desired that the Shallop return next day and bring mattocks and spades with them, since we had forgotten to bring tools.**

Next morning on November 30, we followed certain beaten paths and tracts of the Indians into the woods, supposing they would have led us into some town or houses. After we had gone a while, we lighted upon a very broad beaten path well nigh two foot abroad; concluded we were near their dwellings but in the end, we found it to be only a path made to drive deer in when the Indians hunt. **We marched five or six miles into the woods and could find no signs**

of any people; we returned again another way and found a place like a grave but it was much bigger and longer than any we had seen. We resolved to dig it up, where we found a mat, under that a fair bow and another mat and under that a board three-quarters long, finely carved, and painted with three tynes or broches on the top like a crown. Between the mats, we found bowls, trays, dishes and such like trinkets. Under another mat were two bundles, one containing a quantity of fine and perfect red powder and in it the bones and skull of a man with fine yellow hair still on it; the lesser bundle contained the same powder and the bones and head of a child, legs and other parts, and bracelets of fine white beads. We brought the prettiest things with us and covered corpse again. There were varieties of opinion about the embalmed person. Some thought it an Indian, but Indians have black hair. Others that it was a Christian of special note which had died among them, and they buried him to honor him.

While we were thus ... searching, two sailors, which were newly come ashore, by chance espied two houses which had been lately dwelt in but the people were gone. Hearing no one, they entered the houses and took out some things. The houses were made with long young sapling trees, bended like unto an arbor, and covered down to the ground with thick and well wrought mats. In the houses were found wooden bowls, trays, and dishes, earthen pots, baskets made of crab shells. Also two or three baskets of corn, bundles of flags and sedge and bullrushes and other stuff to make mats. Some of the best things, we took with us. We hasted to the Shallop and got aboard that night. **We intended to leave some things we brought as sign of Peace, but soon as we meet conveniently with them we will give them full satisfaction.** This is our second discovery.

Having discovered this place, it was controversial among us what to do about settling there, some thought best to abide there.

At first, there was a convenient harbour for boats but not ships (being only 12 feet deep). Secondly, good corn ground as we saw by experience by the corn yielded. Thirdly, Cape Cod, a place of good fishing. Fourthly, the place was likely to be healthful, secure and defensible. But last, but now that the heart of winter was come upon us, we could not go upon coasting and discovery without danger of losing men and boat, upon which would follow overthrow of all.

It was also conceived that whilst we had victuals the Ship would stay but when they grew low they would be gone, and let us shift for ourselves.

So others urged greatly the going off to the Northwards which they had heard to be an excellent harbor for Ships; better ground and better shipping.

Secondly, it would be a better settlement, and it would be a hindrance to settle where we shall move again.

Thirdly, the water was but in ponds here, and it was thought there would be none in Summer.

Fourthly, the water must be fetched up a steep hill.

It was in the end concluded to make some discovery within the bay.

Our pilot, Robert Coppin, made relation of a great navigable river and **good harbor** in the other headland of this bay almost right over against Cape Cod, being a right line not much above eight leagues distant in which he had been once. Because one of the wild men with whom they had been trucking stole a harping iron from them, they called it Thievish Harbor. And beyond that place they were enjoyned not to go, whereupon **a company was chosen to go upon a third discovery.**

While some were on this third discovery, it pleased God that Mistress White was brought to bed of a son, which was called Peregrine.

The 5th day [December], we through God's mercy escaped a great danger by a foolishness of a boy, one of John Billington's sons [Francis] who in his father's absence had got into gun powder, and had shot off a piece or two and made squibs, and there being a fowling piece, charged in his father's cabin, shot her off in the cabin there, being a little barrel of powder half full scattered in and about the cabin, the fire, being within four feet of the bed, between decks, and many flints and iron things about the cabin, and many people about the fire, yet by God's mercy no harm done.

Wednesday, the **6th of December** it was resolved, our discoverers should set forth, for the day before was too foul weather.

Ten of our men were appointed who were of themselves

willing to undertake it to wit: Capt. Standish, Master Carver, William Bradford, Edward Winslow, John Tilley, Edward Tilley, John Howland, and three of London, Richard Warren, Stephen Hopkins and Edward Dotte (Doty) and two of our seamen, John Alderton and Thomas English; of the Ship's company, there were two of the Master's Mates - Master Clarke and Master Coppin, the Master gunner and three sailors.

Wednesday, the 6th of December we set out, being very cold and hard weather. We were a long while, after we launched from the Ship before we could get clear of a sandy point which lay within less than a furlong of the same. In which two were very sick - Edward Tilley, and the gunner was also sick unto the death, but hopes of trucking made him to go. And so remained all that day and the next night.

At length we got clear of the Sandy point, and got upon our sails, and within an hour or two we got under the weather shore, and then had smoother water and smoother sailing. But it was very cold for the water froze on our clothes, and made them many times like coats of iron; we sailed six or seven leagues by the shore but saw neither river nor creek; at length we met with a tongue of land, being flat off from the shore with a sandy point. We bore up to gain the point and found a fair income or rode, of a Bay, being a league over at the narrowest and some two or three in length, but we made right over to the land before us, and left the discovery of this income till the next day.

As we drew near shore, we espied some ten or twelve Indians very busy about a black thing. What the black was, we could not tell, till afterwards they saw us and ran to and fro as if they had been carrying something away. We landed a league or two from them, and had much ado to put ashore anywhere, it lay so full of flat sands.

When we came ashore, we made us a Baricado [barricade] and got firewood, and set out our sentinels, and betook us to our lodging, such as it was; we saw the smoke of the fire which the savages made that night, four or five miles from us.

In the morning we divided our company, some 8 in the Shallop, and the rest on shore went to discover this place, but we found it only to be a Bay without either river or creek coming into it. Yet we deemed it to be as good an harbor as Cape Cod for they sounded it, found a Ship might ride in five fathoms of water, we on the land found it to be a level soil but none of the fruitfullest; we saw two becks of fresh water, which were the first running streams we saw in the Country, but one might stride over them. We found also a great fish, called a Grampus, dead on the sands; they in the Shallop found two of them also in the bottom of the bay, dead in like sort; they were cast up at high water, and could not get off for the frost and ice; they were some five or six paces long, and about two inches thick of fat, and fleshed like a Swine; they would have yielded a great deal of oil, if there had been time and means to have taken it, so we finding nothing for our turn, both we and our Shallop returned. We then directed our course along the Sea-sands, to the place where we first saw the Indians; when we were there, we saw it was also a Grampus which they were cutting up; they cut it into long rands or pieces, about an eel long, and two handful broad; we found here and there a piece scattered by the way so it seemed for haste; this place the most were minded we should call Grampus Bay, because we found so many of them there; we followed the tract of the Indians' bare feet a good way on the sands; at length we saw where they struck into the woods by the side of a Pond. As we went to view the place, one said he thought he saw an Indian house among the trees, so went up to see. Here we and the Shallop lost sight one of another till night, it being now about nine or ten o'clock; so we lighted on a path, but saw no house, and followed a great way into the woods: at length we found where corn had been set, but not that year. Anon we found a great burying place, one part whereof was encompassed with a large Palazado, like a Church-yard with long spires four or five yards long, set as close by another as they could, two or three foot in the ground: within it was full of graves, some bigger, and some less, some were also paled about and others had like an Indianhouse made over them, but not matted: those Graves were more sumptuous than those at Cornhill yet we dug none of them up, but only viewed them and went our way; without the Palazado were graves also, but not so costly; from this place we went and found more corn ground, but not of this year. As we ranged we lighted on four or five Indian houses which had been lately dwelt in. There was nothing left but two or three pieces of old mats and baskets of parched acorns hid in the ground.

All this while we saw no people. We went ranging up and down till the sun began to draw low, and then we hasted out of the woods, that we might come to our Shallop which we espied a great way off. We called them to come unto us, which they did as soon as they could, for it was not yet high water.

They were exceeding glad to see us, for they feared because they had not seen us in so long a time. So being both weary and faint for we had eaten nothing all that day, we fell to make our rendez-vous and get firewood which always cost us a great deal of labor.

By the time we had done, and our Shallop came to us, it was within night and we fed upon such victuals as we had, and betook us to our rest, after we had set our watch.

About midnight we heard a great and hideous cry, and our sentinel said, "Arm, arm". So we bestirred ourselves, and set off a couple of muskets and the noise ceased. We concluded that it was a company of wolves or foxes. At 5 o'clock in the morning, we began stirring, and two or three which doubted whether their pieces would go off, made trial of them and shot them off but though at nothing at all.

After prayer, we prepared ourselves for breakfasst and for a journey, and it being now the twilight in the morning, it was thought meet to carry things down to the Shallop. Some said, it was not best to carry the armour down; others said they would be readier, two or three said, they would not carry theirs, till they went themselves, mistrusting nothing at all. As it turned out, the water not being high enough, they laid the things down on the shore and came up to breakfast.

Anon, all upon a sudden, we heard a great and strange cry which we knew to be the same voices though varied their notes. One of our company being abroad, came running in and cried "They are men, Indians". Their arrows came flying among us, and our men ran out withal speed to recover their arms, as by the good Providence of God, they did.

In the meantime Captain Myles Standish, having a snaphance ready, made a shot, and after him, another. After these two had shot, others of us were ready, but he wished us not to shoot till we could take aim, for we knew not what need we should have, and there were four only of us which had their arms ready, and stood before the open side of our Baricado which was first assaulted; they thought it best to defend it, lest the enemy should take it and their stuff, and so have the more advantage against us; our care was no less for the Shallop, but we hoped all the rest would defend it. We called to them to know how well it was with them, and they answered. "Well, well, everyone, and be of good courage". We heard three of their pieces go off, and the rest called for a firebrand to light their matches. One took a log out of the fire on his shoulder, and went and carried it unto them, which was thought did a little to discourage our enemies. The cry of our enemies was dreadful, especially when our men ran out to recover their arms. Their note was after this manner "woach, haha, huch woach." Our men were no sooner come to their arms, but the enemy was ready to assualt them.

There was a lusty man and no wit valiant, who was thought to be their captain, stood behind a tree within half a musket shot of us, and there let his arrows fly at us. He was seen to shoot three arrows which were all avoided for he at whom the first arrow was aimed, saw it, and stooped down, and it flew over him; the rest were avoided also. He stood three shots of a musket, at length; one took, as he said, full aim at him after which he gave an extraordinary cry, and away they, went, all. We followed them about a quarter of a mile but we left 6 to keep our Shallop **for we were careful of our business.** Then we shouted all together several times; and shot off a couple of muskets, and so returned. This we did that they might see we were not afraid of them, nor discouraged.

Thus it pleased God to vanquish our enemies, and give us deliverance. By their noise we could not guess that they were less than thirty or forty, though some thought that they were many more. Yet in the dark of the morning, we could not so well discern them among the trees, as they could see us by our fireside. **We took up 18 of their arrows which we have sent to England by Master Jones.** Some whereof were headed with brasse, others with Hart's horne, and others with Eagles claws. Many more no doubt were shot, as these we found were almost covered with leaves.

Yet **by the especial providence of God; none of them either hit or hurt us,** though many came close by us and on every side of us; and some coats which hung up in our Baricade were shot through and through. So after we had given God thanks for our deliverance, we took our Shallop, and went on our Journey, and called this place, **The First Encounter.**

From thence, we intended to have sailed to the aforesaid Thievish Harbor, if we found us convenient Harbor by the way. Having the wind good, we sailed all that day along the coast about 15 leagues, but saw neither river nor creek to put into.

After we had sailed an hour or two, it began to snow and rain and to be bad weather. About the midst of the afternoon, the wind increased, and the seas began to be very rough, and the hinges of the rudder broke so that we could steer no longer with it, but two men with much ado were fain to serve with a couple of oars. The seas were grown go great that we were much troubled and in great danger, and night grew on. Anon Master Coppin bade us be of good cheer, as he saw the Harbor. As we drew near, the gale being stiff, and we bearing great sail to get, split our mast in three pieces, and were like to have cast away our Shallop. Yet by God's mercy, recovering ourselves, we had the flood with us and struck into the harbor, that day being Saturday, December 9.

Now he that thought that had been the place, was deceived, it being a place where not any of us had been before. Coming into the Harbor, he that was our Pilot did bear up northward, which if we had continued, we had been cast away. Yet, still the Lord kept us, and **we bare up for an land before us** and recovering of that land, **being compassed about with many Rocks,** and dark night brewing upon us, it pleased the Divine providence that we fell upon a place of Sandy ground, where our Shallop did ride safe and secure all that night; and coming upon a strange land kept our watch all night in the rain upon that land. In the morning we marched about it, and found no inhabitants at all, and here made our rendezvous all that day, being Saturday, December 9.

... December 10, on the Sabbath day, we rested, and on Monday, December 11, we sounded the harbor and found it a very good Harbor for our Shipping. We marched also, into the land, and found divers cornfields and little running brooks, a place very good for our situation **so we returned to our Ship again with good news for the rest which did much comfort our hearts.**

On the 15th of December we weighed anchor to go to the place we had discovered, and coming within two leagues of the land we could not fetch the harbor, but were fain to put room again towards Cape Cod, our course lying west. The wind was at northwest, but it pleased God that the next day being Saturday, **the 16th day,** the wind came fair, and we put to sea again and came safely into a **safe harbor.** Within a half hour the wind changed, so as if we had been letted but a little, we had gone back to Cape Cod.

This Harbor is a greater bay than Cape Cod, compassed with a goodly land. The fine lands are uninhabited, wherein are nothing but wood, oaks, pines, walnut, beech, sassifras and others we know not.

The Bay is a most hopeful place, innumerable store of fowl and excellent good, and cannot but be of fish in their season: skote, cod, turbot and herring, we have tasted of; abundance of mussels, the greatest and best we ever saw, crabs and lobsters, in their time, infinite.

Monday, the 18th, we went aland manned with the master of the Ship and 3 or 4 sailors; we marched along the coast in the woods some 7 or 8 miles but we saw not an Indian nor an Indian house, only we found where formerly had been some inhabitants, and where they had planted their corn. We found not any navigable river, but 4 or 5 small running brooks of very **sweet fresh water** that all run into the Sea. The land for the crust of the earth is a spits depth, excellent black mold and fat in some places 2 or 3 great oaks but not very thick. Pines, walnuts, beech, ash, birch, hasell, holly, asp, sassafras in abundance and vines everywhere, cherry trees and many others which we know not. Many kinds of herbs, we found here in Winter as strawberry leaves innumberable. Sorrell, yarow, carnell, brook-line, liverwort, watercresses, great store of licks and onions, and an excellent strong kind of flax and hemp. Here is sand, gravel and excellent clay, no better in the world, excellent for pots and will wash like soap, and a great store of stone, though somewhat soft, and the best water that ever we drank, and the brooks now begun to be full of fish. **That night many being weary with marching, we went aboard again.**

The next morning, being Tuesday **the 19th of December, we went again to discover further, some went on land and some went in the Shallop.**

The land we found, as the former day we did, and we found a creek, and went up three English miles, a very pleasant river; at full sea a bark of thirty ton may go up, but at low water scarce our Shallop could pass. This place we had a great liking to plant in. But that it was so far from our fishing, our principal profit, and so encompassed with woods that we should be much in danger of savages. Our number being so little, and so much ground to clear so as we thought good to quit, and clear that place till we were of more strength.

Some of us having a good mind for safety to plant in the greater Ile [Clark's Island], we crossed the Bay which there is five or six miles over and found the Ile about a mile and a half or two miles about all wooded, and no fresh water but 2 or 3 pits that doubted of fresh water in summer, and so full of wood, as we could hardly clear so much as to serve us for corn, besides we judged it cold for our corn, and some part very rocky. Yet divers thought it as a place and of great security.

That night, December 19, we returned again ashipboard with resolution the next morning to settle on some of those places. So in **the next morning after we had called on God for direction, we came to this resolution to go presently ashore again, and to take a better view of two places which we thought most fitting for us for we could not now take time for further search** or consideration, our victuals being much spent, especially our deer, and it being now the 19th of December.

After our landing and viewing of the places, so well as we could **we came to a conclusion by most voices to set on the main Land on the first place on high ground where there is a great deal of land cleared and hath been planted with corn 3 or 4 years ago.** There is a very sweet brook runs under the hillside, and many delicate springs of as good water as can be drunk, and where we may harbor our Shallops exceedingly well, and in this brook much good fish in their season. On the further side also much good corn ground cleared. In one field is a great hill on which to make a platform and plant our ordinance, which will command all round about. From thence, we can see into the Bay and far into the Sea, and we may see then Cape Cod.

Our greatest labor will be fetching of our wood which is half a quarter of an English mile, but there is enough so far off. What people are inhabited here we yet know not for as yet we have seen none. So there we made our rendezvous and a place for our people, about twenty resolving in the morning to all come ashore and build houses.

But the morning being Thursday, the 21st of December, it was stormy and wet that we could not go ashore, and those that remained there all night could do nothing but were wet, not having daylight enough to make them a sufficient court of guard to keep them dry. All that night it blew and rained extremely; it was so tempestuous, that the Shallop could not go on land so soon as was meet, for they had no victuals on land. About 11 o'clock the Shallop went off with much ado with provisions, but could not return as it blew so strong and was such foul weather, that we were forced to let fall our anchor and ride with three anchors ahead.

Friday, December 22, the storm still continued, that we could not get a-land, nor they come to us aboard.

This morning good wife Allerton was delivered of a son, but dead born.

Saturday, the 23rd, so many of us as could went on shore, felled and carried timber, to provide themselves stuff for building.

Sunday, the 24th, our people on shore heard a cry of some savages, as they thought, which caused an alarm and to stand on their guard, expecting an assault but all was quiet.

Monday, the 25th, we went on shore, some to fell timber, some to saw, some to rive and some to carry, so no man rested all that day. But towards night some, as they were at work, heard a noise of some Indians which caused us all to go to our muskets, but we heard no further, so we came aboard again, and left some twenty to keep the court of guard. That night we had a sore storm of wind and rain.

Monday, the 25, being Christmas day, we began to drink water aboard. But at night Master Jones caused us to have some beer, and so on board, we had diverse times, now and then some beer, but on shore none at all.

Tuesday the 26th it was fowl weather, that we could not go ashore.

Wednesday December 27 we went to work again.

Thurday, the 28th of December, so many as went to work on the hill where we purposed to build our platform for our ordinance, and which doth command all the plain and the Bay and from whence we may see far into the Sea. And might be easier impaled, having two rows of houses and a fair street.

So in the afternoon we went to measure out the grounds. First we took notice how many families there were; willing all single men, that had no wives, to join with some family as they thought fit, so we might build fewer houses, which was done, and we reduced them to 19 families. To greater families we allotted larger plots. To every person a half a pole (square rod) in breadth and three in length. So lots were cast where every man should lie which was done and staked out. **We thought this proportion was large enough at first for houses and gardens to impale them around, considering the weakness of our people many of them growing ill with colds from our discoveries in frost and storms, and the wading at Cape Cod had brought much weakness amongst us** which increased so every day more and more, and after was the cause of many of their deaths.

Friday and Saturday we fitted ourselves for our labor but our people on shore were much troubled and discouraged with rain and wet, that day being very stormy and cold.

We saw great smokes of fire made by the Indians about six or seven miles from us, as we conjectured.

Monday, the first of January, we went to work. We were much hindered in lying so far off from the land, and fain to go as the tide served that we lost much time for our Ship drew so much water that she lay a mile and a half off though a Ship of 70 or 80 ton at high water may come to the shore.

Wednesday, the **third of January, some of our people being abroad to get and gather thatch, they saw great fires of the Indians** and were at their cornfields, yet saw none of the savages nor had seen any of them since we came to this Bay.

Thursday, the 4th of January, Captain Myles Standish, with four or five more went to see if they could meet with any of the savages in that place where fires were made; they went to some of their houses but not lately inhabited, yet they could not meet any. As they came home they **shot an eagle** and killed her which was excellent meat - it was hardly to be discerned from mutton.

Friday, the 5th of January, one of the sailors found alive upon the shore an herring which the Master [Jones] had for supper which put us in hope of fish but as yet we had got but one cod.

Saturday, the 6th of January, Master Martin (the treasurer) was very sick, and to our judgement no hope of life, so Master Carver was sent for to come aboard to speak with him about his accounts, who came next morning.

Monday, the 8th of January, was a very fair day, and we went betimes to work. Master Jones sent the Shallop as he had formerly done to see where fish could be got. They had a great storm at sea, and were in some danger. At night they returned with three great seals and an excellent good cod, which did assure us that we should have plenty of fish shortly.

The same day Francis Billington having the week before seen from the top of a tree on a high hill a great sea, as he thought, went with one of the masters mates to see it. They went three miles, and then came to a great water, divided into two great lakes, the bigger of them five or six miles in circuit and in it an Ile of a cable length square, the other three miles in compass, in their estimation. They are fine fresh water full of fish and fowl. A brook issues from it. It will be an excellent help for us in time. They found 7 or 8 Indian houses but not lately inhabited. When they saw the Indian houses, they were in some fear, for they were but two persons and one piece.

Tuesday, the 9th of January was a reasonably fair day, and we went to labor that day in the building of our town in two rows of houses for safety. We divided by lot the plot of ground whereon to build our own.

After the proportion formerly allotted **we agreed that every man should build his own house thinking by that course, men would make more haste than working in common.**

The common house, in which for the first, we made our rendezvous, being near finished, wanted only covering, it being about 20 foot square. Some would make mortar, and some gather thatch, so that in four days half of it was thatched. Frost and fowl weather hindered us much. This time of year seldom could we work half the week.

Thursday, the 11th, William Bradford being at work, it was a fair day, was vehemently taken with a grief and pain and so shot to his knuckle bone. It was doubted that he would have instantly died. He got cold in the former discoveries [expeditions], especially the last, and felt some pain in his ankles by times but he grew a little better towards night, and in time, through God's mercy in the use of means, recovered.

Friday, January 12, we went to work, but about noon, it began to rain that it forced us to give over work.

This day two of our people put us in great sorrow and care. There were four sent together, and cut thatch in the morning. Two of them John Goodman and Peter Browne having cut thatch all forenoon went to a further place, and willed the other two to bind up that which was cut, and to follow them.

So they did, being about a mile and a half from our Plantation, but when the two came after, they couldn't find them nor hear anything of them at all though they hallowed and shouted as loud as they could. So they returned to the company, and told them of it.

Whereupon Master Carver and three or four more went to seek them but could hear nothing of them, so they returning, sent more but that night they could hear nothing at all of them. The next day they armed 10 or 12 men out verily thinking the Indians had surprised them. They went seeking 7 or 8 miles, but could neither see or hear anything at all, so they returned with much discomfort to us all.

These, too, that were missed at dinner time took their meat in their hands and would go walk and refresh themselves. So going a little off, they found a lake of water, and having a great mastif bitch with them and a spaniel. By the waterside, they found a great deer. The dogs chased him, and they followed him so far, as they lost themselves, and could not find the way back. They wandered all that afternoon, being wet, and that night it did freeze and snow. They were slenderly apparelled, and had no weapons but each his own sickle nor any victuals. They ranged up and down, and could find none of the savages habitations.

When they drew nigh, they were much perplexed, for they could find neither harbor nor meat. But in the frost and snow were forced to make the earth their bed and the element their covering.

And another thing did much terrify them, they heard, as they thought, two lions roaring exceedingly for a long time together, and a third then thought was very near them.

So not knowing what to do, they resolved to climb up into a tree as their safest refuge, though that would prove an intolerable cold lodging. So they stood at the tree's root, so that when the lions came they might take their opportunity of climbing up. The bitch they were feign to hold by the neck, for she would have gone to the lion. But it pleased God, so to dispose that the wild beasts came not so. So they walked up and down under the tree all night. It was an extreme cold night. So soon as it was light, they traveled again, passing by many lakes and brooks and woods, and in one place where the Savages had burnt the space of five miles in length, which is a fine champion country and even ground.

In the afternoon it pleased God from an high hill, they discovered the two Iles in the Bay so that night got to the Plantation, being ready to faint with travail, and for want of victuals, and almost famished with cold. John Goodman was fain to have his shoes cut off his feet, they were so swelled with cold, and it was a long while after ere he was able to go. Those on the shore were much comforted at their return, but they on shipboard, were grieved, as deeming them lost.

But the next day, being the 14th of January, in the morning about 6 of the clock, they on shipboard spied their great new rendezvous on fire, which was to them a new discomfort, fearing because of the supposed loss of the men, that the savages had fired them. Neither could they presently go to them for want of water, but after three quarters of an hour, they went as they purposed the day before, to keep the Sabbath on shore, because now there was the greater number of people.

At their landing they heard good tidings of the return of the two men, and that the house was fired by a spark that flew into the thatch, which instantly burned it all up, but the roof stood and little hurt.

The most loss was Master Carver's and William Bradford's, who then lay sick in bed, and if they had not risen with good speed, had been blown up with powder. But through God's mercy they had no harm. The house was as full of beds as they could lie one by another, and their muskets charged, but blessed be God there was no harm done.

Monday, the 15th day of January, it rained much all day, that they on shipboard could not go on shore, nor they on shore, do any labor, but were all wet.

Tuesday, Wednesday, Thursday were very fair sunshine days, as if it had been in April, and **our people so many as were in health wrought cheerfully.**

The 19th day, we resolved to make a shed to put our common provision in, of which some were already set on shore, but at noon it rained that we could not work.

This day in the evening John Goodman went abroad for a walk to use his lame feet that were pitifully ill with the cold he had got, having his little Spaniel with him. A little way from the Plantation, two great wolves ran after the dog. The dog ran to his master, and betwixt his legs for succour. He had nothing in his hand, but took up a stick and threw at one of them, and hit him and they presently both ran away, but came again. He got a pail board in his hand, and they sat both on their tails, grinning at him a good while, and went their way and left him.

Saturday, the 20th of January, **we made up our shed for our common goods.**

Sunday, the 21st, we kept our meeting on land.

Monday, the 22nd, was a fair day. We wrought on our houses, and in the afternoon carried up our hog's head of meal to our common store house.

The rest of the week we followed our business likewise.

Monday, January 29, in the morning, cold frost and sleet, but afternoon reasonably fair. Both long boat and the Shallop brought our common goods on shore.

Tuesday and Wednesday 30 and 31 of January, cold frosty weather, and sleet, that we could not work. In the morning the Master Jones and others saw two savages, that had been on the land near our Ship. What they came for, we could not tell. They were going so far back again, before they were descried that we could not speak with them.

Sunday, the 4th of February, was very wet, and rainy with the greatest gusts of wind, that ever we had since we came forth. That though we rode in a very good harbor, yet we were in danger, because our Ship was light, the goods taken out, and she unballasted. It caused much daubing of our houses to fall down.

Friday, the 9th, still the cold weather continued, and we could do little work. That afternoon, our little house for our sick people, set on fire, by a spark that kindled in the roof, but no great harm done.

That evening Master Jones going ashore killed five geese, which he friendly distributed among the sick people. He found also a good deer killed, the savages had cut off the horns, and a wolf was eating of him. How he came there he could not conceive.

Friday, February the 16th, was a fair day but the northernly wind continued which continued the frost. This day afternoon, one of our people being afouling, and having taken a stand by a creek side in the reeds about a mile and a half from our plantation, there came by him 2 Indians, and in the woods he heard the noise of many more. He lay close till they were passed, and then with what speed he could he went home, and gave the alarm, so the people abroad in the woods returned, and armed themselves but saw none of them; only toward evening they made a great fire about the place where they were first discovered. Captain Myles Standish and Francis Cooke, being at work in the woods, coming home, left their tools behind them, but before they returned, their tools were taken away by the savages.

Wednesday, the 7th of March, the wind was full east, cold but fair. **That day Master Carver with five others went to the great ponds which seem to be excellent fishing places.** All the way they went, they found it exceedingly beaten, and haunted with deer, but they saw none. They saw one, a milk white fowl with a very black head. This day some garden seed were sown.

Friday, the 16th, a fair warm day. **This morning we determined to conclude of the military orders which we had begun to consider of before,** but were interrupted by the savages, as we mentioned formerly. And whilst, we were busy hereabouts, we were interrupted again for presented himself a savage, which caused alarm. He very boldly came all alone, and along the houses straight to the rendezvous, where we intercepted him, not suffering him to go in, as undoubtedly he would out of his boldness. He saluted us in English, and bade us welcome. For he had learned some broken English, amongst some of the English men that came to fish at Monhegan, and knew most of the captains, commanders and masters that usually came.

He was a man free in speech, so far as he could express his mind, and of a seemly carriage. We questioned him of many things. He was the first savage we could meet withal.

He said he was not of these parts, but of Morattigan, and one of the Sagamores or lords thereof, and had been eight months in these parts. It lying hence a day's sail with a great wind, and five days by land. He discoursed of the whole country, and of every province, and of their Sagamores, and their number of men and strength. The wind being to rise a little, we cast a horseman's coat about him, for he was stark naked, only a leather about his waist with a fringe about a span long or little more. He had a bow and two arrows, the one headed, and the other unheaded. He was a tall straight man, the hair of his head black, long behind only short before, none on his face at all.

He asked for some beer, but we gave him strong water, and bisket and butter and cheese, and pudding, and a piece of mallard, all which he liked well, and had been acquainted with such amongst the English.

He told us the place where we now live is called Patuxet and that about four years ago all the inhabitants died of an extraordinary plague, and there is neither man, woman, nor child remaining, as indeed we have found none. So there is none to hinder our possession or to lay claim unto it. All the afternoon, we spent in communication with him. We would gladly have been rid of him at night, but he was not willing to go this night. Then we thought to carry him on ship-board, he was well content, and went into the Shallop, but the wind was high, and water scant, that it could not return back. We lodged him that night at Stephen Hopkins' house, and watched him.

The next day he went away back to the Massasoits, from whence he said he came, who are our next bordering neighbors. They are 60 strong, as he said. The Nausets are as near Southeast of them, and are a hundred strong. Those were they of whom our people were encountered, as we before related. They are much incensed, and provoked against the English. About eight months ago slew three Englishmen, and two more hardly escaped by flight to Monhegan, as this Savage told us. It was the Nausets, our discoverers had the fight with. And about our tools that were taken out of the woods, we willed him they should be brought back, or we would fight ourselves.

These people are ill affected towards the English, by reason of one Hunt, Master of a Ship, who deceived the people, and got them under color of trucking with them, twenty out of this very place, where we inhabited, and seven from the Nausets. He carried them away, and sold them for slaves, like a wretched man, for 20 pounds a man, that cares not what mischief he does for his profit.

Saturday in the morning, we dismissed the Savage, and gave him a knife, a bracelet, and a ring. He promised within a night or two to come again, and bring with him some of the Massasoits, our neighbors, with such bear skins as they had to trade.

This coming of the Savages gave us occasion to keep more strict watch, and to make our pieces and furniture ready, which by the moisture and rain were out of temper.

Saturday, the 17th day in the morning **we called a meeting for the establishing of military orders amongst ourselves, and we chose Myles Standish our captain and gave him authority of command in affairs. And as we were in consultation hereabouts, two Savages presented themselves** upon the top of an hill over against our Plantation about a quarter of a mile and less, and made signs unto us to come to them.

We, likewise, made signs unto them to come to us, where upon we armed ourselves, and stood ready, and sent two over the brook towards them, to wit, Captain Standish and Stephen Hopkins. They went towards the Indians; only one of them had a musket, which they laid down on the ground in their sight, in sign of peace, and to parley with them.

But the savages would not tarry their coming. A noise of a great many more was heard behind the hill, but no more came in sight. This caused us to plant our great ordnance in places most convenient.

Wednesday, the 21st of February, the Master [Jones) came on shore with many of his sailors, and brought with him one of the great pieces, called a minion, and helped us draw it up a hill with another piece that lay on shore, and mounted them, and a cellar, and two bases. He brought with him a very fat goose to eat with us, and we had a fat crane, and a mallard, and a dried neats-tongue, and so we were kindly and friendly together.

Saturday, the third of March, the wind was south, the morning misty, but towards noon, warm and fair weather. The birds sang in the woods most pleasantly. At 1 o'clock, it thundered, which was the first we heard in that country. It was strong and great claps, but short; after an hour, it rained very sadly till midnight.

Saturday and Sunday were reasonable fair days.

On this day came again the Savage, and brought with him five other tall and proper men. They had every man a deerskin on him, and the principal of them had a wild cat's skin or such like on the one arm. They have most of them hose on up to their groins, close made. Above their groins to their waist another leather. They were altogether like the Irish trousers. They are of complexion like our English gypsies - no hair or very little hair on their faces, on their heads long hair to their shoulders, only cut before, some trussed up before with a feather, broadwise like a fan, another, a fox tail hanging out. These left, according to our charge given him before, their bows and arrows a quarter of a mile from our town.

We gave them entertainment, as we thought was fitting them. They did eat liberally of our English victuals. **They made semblance unto us of friendship and amity.** They sang and danced, after their manner, like anticks. They brought with them in a thing like a bowcase (which the principal of them had about his waist) a little of the corn powdered to powder which mixed with a little water they eat. He had a little tobacco in a bag, but none of them drank, but when, he listed. Some of them had their faces painted black from the forehead to the chin, four or five fingers abroad. Others, after other fashions, as they liked. They brought three or four skins, but we would not trade with them that day, but wished them to bring more, and we would trade for all.

They promised to return within a night or two, and would leave these skins behind, though we were not willing they should. They also returned our tools which were taken in the woods, in our men's absence. So because of the day [Sunday], we dismissed them, as soon as we could.

But Samoset, our first acquaintance, either was sick or feigned himself so, and would not go with them, and stayed with us till Wednesday morning. Then we sent him to them to know the reason they came not, according to their words. We gave him a hat, a pair of stockings and shoes, a shirt and a piece of cloth to tie about his waist.

The Sabbath day when we sent them from us, we gave every one of them some trifles, especially the principal of them. We escorted them along with our arms to the place where they left their bows and arrows, whereat they were amazed, and the two of them began to slink away, but the others called them. When they took their arrows, we bade them farewell, and they were glad, and so with many thanks given us, they departed with promise they would come again.

Monday and Tuesday proved fair days, we dug grounds and sowed.

Wednesday a fine warm day, we sent away Samoset.

That day we had again a meeting to conclude of laws and orders for ourselves, and to confirm those military orders, that were formerly propounded and twice broken off by the savages coming. But so we were again the third time, for after we had been an hour together, on the top of the hill over against us, two or three savages presented themselves, that made semblance of daring us, as we thought. So Captain Standish with another with their muskets went over to them with two of the Master's mates, and rubbed their arrows, and string, and made show of defiance, but when our men drew near them, they ran away. Thus we were again interrupted by them.

This day with much ado we got our carpenter that had been long sick of the scurvey **to fit our Shallop and to fetch all from aboard ship.**

Thursday, the 22nd of March was a very fair, warm day. About noon we met again about our public business, but Samoset came again, and Squanto, the only native of Patuxet, where we now inhabited who was one of the 20 captives that by Hunt were carried away, and had been in England, and dwelt in Cornhill with Master John Slanie, a merchant, and could speak a little English with three others. They brought with them some few skins to trade, and some red herrings, newly taken and dried, but not salted, and signified unto us that their great Sagamore Massasoit was hard by with Quadiquina, his brother, and all their men.

They could not well express in English what they would, but after an hour the King came to the top of the hill over against us, and had in his train 60 men, that we could well behold, and they us.

We were not willing to send our Governor to them, and they unwilling to come to us, so Squanto went again unto him who brought word that we should send one to parley with him which we did, which was Edward Winslow, to know his mind, and **to signify the mind and will of our Governor, which was to have trading and peace with him.**

We sent to the King a pair of knives, and a copper chain with a Jewel in it. To Quadiquina we sent, likewise, a knife, and a jewel to hang in his ear, and withal a pot of strong water, and a good quantity of biscuit and some butter, which were all willingly accepted. Our messenger made a speech unto him, that King James saluted him with words of love and peace, and did accept him as his friend and ally, and that **our Governor desired to see him and to trade with him and confirm Peace with him as his Next Neighbor.** He liked well of the speech, and heard it attentively, though the Interpreters did not well express it. After he had eaten and drunk himself, and given the rest to his company, he looked upon our messengers sword and armour which he had on, with intimation of his desire to buy it, but on the other side, our messenger shewed his unwillingness to part with it.

In the end, he left him in the custody of his brother, Quadequina and came over the brook, and some twenty men following him, leaving all their bows and arrows behind them.

We kept 6 or 7 as hostages for our messenger. Captain Standish and Master Williamson met the King at the brook with a half dozen musketeers. They saluted him, and he them, so one going over, the one on the one side, and the other on the other, conducted him to a house, then in a building, where we placed a green rug, and 3 or 4 cushions. Then instantly came our Governor with drum and trumpet after him, and some few musketeers.

After saluations, our Governor kissing his hand, the King kissed him, and so they sat down. The Governor called for some strong water [this was probably Metheglin, a drink made by the Pilgrims of herbs and fermented honey with water] and drank to him, then Massasoit drank a great draught that made him sweat all the while after. He called for a little fresh meat which the King did eat willingly, and did give his followers.

Then they treated of Peace which was:

1. That neither he nor any of his should injure or do hurt to any of our people.

2. And if any of his did hurt to any of ours, he should send the offender that we might punish him.

3. That if any of our tools were taken away when our people were at work, he should cause them to be restored, and if ours did any harm to any of his, we should do the like to them.

4. If any did unjustly war against him we would aid him. If any did war against us, he should aid us.

5. He should send to his neighbor[ing] confederates to certify them of this, that they might not wrong us, but might be likewise comprised in the condition of Peace.

6. That when their men came to us, they should leave their bows and arrows behind them, as we should do our pieces when we came to them.

Lastly, that doing thus, King James would esteem of him as his friend and ally: all which the King seemed to like well, and it was applauded of his followers. **All the while, he sat by the Governor he trembled for fear.** In his person he is a very lusty man, in his best years, an able body grave of, and spare of speech. In his attire little or nothing differing from the rest of his followers, only in a great chain of white bone beads about his neck, and on it behind his neck hangs a little bag of tobacco which he drank and gave us to drink [they mixed it with water and sipped it]. His face was painted with a sad red, like murry, and oiled, both head and face, that he looked greasily. All his followers, likewise, were in their faces, in part or in whole painted, some black, some red, some yellow and some white, some with crosses, and other antic works. Some had skins on them, and some naked, all strong, tall, all men in appearance. So after all was done, **the Governor conducted him to the brook and there embraced each other and he departed.** We, diligently keeping our hostages, we expected our messenger coming, but anon word was brought us that Quadiquina was coming, and our messenger was stayed till his return, who presently came, and a troop with him. So likewise, we entertained him, and conveyed him to the place prepared. He was very fearful of our pieces, and made signs of dislike, that they should be carried away. He was a very proper, tall young man, of a modest and seemly countenance, and he did kindly like our entertainment, so we conveyed him likewise, as we did the King, but divers of their people stayed still. When he was returned then, they dismissed our messenger.

Two of his people would have stayed all night, but we would not suffer it. One thing I forgot, the King had in his bosom hanging in a string a great long knife. He marvelled much at our trumpet, and some of his men would sound it, as well as they could.

Samoset and Squanto stayed all night with us, and the King and all his men lay all night in the woods, not about half an English mile from us, and all their wives and women with them.

They said that within eight or nine days they would come and set corn on the other side of the brook, and dwell there all summer which is hard by us.

That night we kept good watch, but there was no appearance

of danger. The next morning divers of their people came over to us, hoping to get some victuals as we imagined. Some of them told us the King would have some of us come see him. Captain Standish and Isaac Allerton went venturesomely who were welcomed of him, after their manner. He gave them three or four ground nuts and some tobacco. We cannot yet conceive, but that he is willing to have Peace with us, for they have seen our people, sometime alone, two or three in the woods at work, and fowling, when as they offered them no harm, as they might easily have done. Especially, because he hath a potent adversary, the Narrogansetts, that are at war with him, against whom he thinks we may be some strength to him, for our pieces are terrible unto them.

This morning they stayed till ten or eleven o'clock, and our Governor bid them send the King's Kettle, and filled it full of peas which pleased them well, and so they went their way.

Friday, March 23 was a very fair day. Samoset and Squanto still remained with us. Squanto went at noon to fish for eels. At night he came home with as many as he could well lift in one hand, which our people were glad of.

This day we proceeded on with our common business from which we had been so often hindered by the Savages coming, and concluded both of military orders, and of some Laws and Orders, as we thought behoofeful for our present estate, and condition, and did likewise choose our Governor for this year, which was Master Carver, a man well approved amongst us.

Part Three

They Broke the Ice for Others

William Bradford,
Of Plymouth Plantation,
Chapters XII–XXI

*"Let it not be grievous unto you that you have been instruments
to break the ice for others who come after with less difficulty; the honor
shall be yours to the world's end."*

From a letter of Their Sponsors

XII   The Mayflower departs, and Corn planted; Governor John Carver Dies of Sunstroke

William Bradford - Anno Domini 1621

They now began to dispatch the Ship away which brought them over, which lay till about this time on the beginning of April [April 5, and arrived in England May 6]. The reason on their part why she stayed so long was the necessity and danger that lay upon them; for it was well towards the end of December before she could land anything ashore. Afterwards, the 14th of January, the house which they had made for a general rendezvous by casualty fell afire, and some were fain to retire aboard for shelter; then the sickness began to fall sore amongst them, and the weather was so bad that they could not make much sooner any dispatch. Again, the Governor and chief of them, seeing so many die, and fall down sick daily, thought it no wisdom to send away the Ship, their condition considered, and the danger they stood in from the Indians, till they could procure some shelter; and therefore, thought it better to draw some more charge upon ourselves and friends than hazard all.

... [At this time], they, as many as were able, began to plant their corn, in which service, Squanto stood them in great stead, showing them both the manner how to set it, and after how to dress and tend it. Also, he told them except they got fish and set with it in these old grounds, it would come to nothing.

In the month of April whilst they were busy about their seed, their Governor, Mr. John Carver, came out of the field very sick, it being a hot day. He complained greatly of his head and lay down, and within a few hours his senses failed, so he never spoke more till he died, which was in days after. Whose death was much lamented and caused great heaviness amongst them as there was cause. He was buried in the best manner they could, with some vollies of shot by all who bore arms. And his wife being a weak woman, died within five or six weeks after him.

Shortly after, William Bradford was chosen governor in his stead, and being not recovered of his illness, in which he had been near the point of death, Isaac Allerton was chosen to be an assistant to him, who, by renewed election every year, continued sundry years together.

The first Thanksgiving

They began now to gather in the small harvest they had, and to fit up their houses and dwellings against winter, being all well recovered in health and strength, and had all things in good plenty. For as some were thus employed in affairs abroad, others were exercised in fishing about cod and bass and other fish, of which they took good store and, of which every family had their portion. All the summer there was not want, and now began to come in a store of fowl, as winter approached, of which this place did abound when they first came, but afterwards decreased by degrees. And besides water fowl, there was a great store of wild turkeys, of which they took many, besides venison, etc. Also, they had a peck of meal a week to a person, and since harvest, Indian corn to that proportion. Which made so many afterwards write so largely of their plenty here to their friends in England, that were not feigned but true reports.

[Edward Winslow's letter of December 11, 1621 to a friend in England, describing this First Thanksgiving, is printed in *Mourt's Relation*:

"Our harvest being gotten in our Governor sent four men on fowling, so we might after a more special manner rejoice together, after we had gathered the fruit of our labors. They, four, in one day killed as much fowl as with a little help beside, served the company almost a week. At which time amongst other recreations, we exercised our arms, many of the Indians coming amongst us, and amongst the rest their greatest King Massasoit with some 90 men, whom for three days we entertained and feasted. And they went out and killed five deer which they brought to the Plantation, and bestowed on our Governor, and upon the Captain and others".]

The Arrival of the Fortune

In November about twelve month that themselves came, there came in a small ship to them unexpected or looked for in which (arrived) Mr. Cushman, so much spoken of before, and with him thirty-five persons to remain and live in the Plantation; which did not a little rejoice them. And when they came ashore, and found all well, and saw plenty of victuals in every house, were not less glad; for most of them were lusty young men, and many of them wild enough, who little considered whither or about what they went, till they came into the harbor at Cape Cod, and there saw nothing but a naked and barren place. They then began to think what should become of them, if the people were dead or cut off by the Indians. [The *Fortune* tarried about three weeks at Provincetown Harbor before proceeding to Plymouth]

... The Plantation was glad of this addition of strength, but could have wished that many of them had been of better condition, and all of them better furnished with provisions.

[Among the 35 passengers were John Adams, Jonathan Brewster, Philip Delano and Thomas Prence.]

In the Ship [*Fortune*] Thomas Weston sent a large letter to Mr. Carver, the late governor, full of complaints ... "Keeping the Ship [*Mayflower*] so long in the country and returning her without lading ... for I am well assured had they [the Adventurers] known as much as I do, on the alterations of the conditions first agreed on between us, they would not have adventured a half a penny of what was necessary for this Ship. That you sent no lading is wonderful and worthily distasted. I know your weakness was the cause of it, and I believe more weakness of judgement than of hands.

"If you mean, bona fide, to perform the conditions agreed upon, do us the favour to copy them out fair, and subscribe them with the principal of your names ... the life of the business depends on the lading of this Ship, which if you do to any good purpose, so that I may be freed from the great sums I have disbursed for the former and must do for the latter, I promise I will never quit the business, though all the Adventurers should.

"We have procured a charter, the best we could which is better than your former and with less limitation" [to take the place of patent from Virginia Company – original document is in Pilgrim Hall, Plymouth, Massachusetts].

This Ship [the *Fortune*] was speedily dispatched away on December 13, 1621.

[On the day before, December 12, Robert Cushman delivered the first sermon on American soil "The Sin and Danger of Self Love". It is not included by Bradford, but we thought it appropriate to add it at this point in part.

It was printed in London in 1622 but without his name. It discourses on the need of a public spirit in the colonists. The text of the sermon is from I Corinthians X: 24, "Let no man seek his own, but every man another's wealth". A preliminary dissertation invokes his own countrymen who may wish to adventure to the colony:

> *For men who have a large heart and look after great riches, I would not advise them to go there, for as yet the country will afford no such matters. But if there be any such who are content to lay out their estates, spend their time, labours and endeavors for the benefit of them that shall come after, and desire to further the Gospel among those poor heathens, quietly contenting themselves with such hardships and difficulties as by God's providence shall fall upon them .. such men I would advise and encourage to go, for their ends cannot fail them.*

> *... If any marvel at the publishing of this treatise in England ... let them know that the special end is that we keep those motives in memory of ourselves and those that shall come after to be a remedy against self-love, the bane of all societies.*

And from the sermon in America:

It wonderfully encourageth men in their duties when they see the burden equally borne, but when some withdraw themselves, and return to their own particular ease, pleasure, or profit what heart can men have to go on in their business.

When men are come together to lift some weighty piece of timber, if one does not lift, shall not the rest be weakened and disheartened? Will not a few idle drones spoil the whole stock of laborious bees? So one idle belly, one murmurer, one complainer, one self-lover, will weaken and dishearten a whole colony.

Where every man seeks himself, all cometh to nothing.

It is here as it were the dawning of the new world. It is now, therfore, no time for men to look to get riches, brave clothes, dainty fare, but to look to present necessities. It is now no time to pamper the flesh, live at ease, snatch, catch, scrape, and pill and hoard up; but rather to open the doors, the chests and vessels and say: "Brother, neighbor, friend, what want ye? Anything I have? ... It is yours ... to do you good, to comfort and cherish you; and glad I am that I have it for you."

Let there be no prodigal person to come forth and say "Give me the portion of lands and goods that appertaineth to me and let me shift for myself." ... It is yet too soon to put men to their shifts. Why wouldst thou have thy particular portion but because thou thinkest to live better than thy neighbor, and scornest to live so meanly as he?

Nothing in this world doth more resemble heavenly happiness than for men to live as one, being of one heart and soul; neither does anything more resemble hellish horror than for every man to shift for himself; for it be a good mind and practice thus to affect particulars, mine and thine, then it would be best also for God to provide one heaven for thee, and another for thy neighbor.

... All men have not the strength, skill, faculty, spirit and courage to work alike.

As you are a body together, so hang not together by skins and gymocks, but labor to be jointed together, and knit by flesh and sinews. Away with envy. If you profess friendship, be friends in adversity for then a friend is known and tried and not before.

... Bear ye one another's burdens. Avoid all factions, singularity, and cleave fast to the Lord and one another continually; so shall you be a notable precedent to those poor heathens whose eyes are upon you and who ... cruelly do daily consume one another through wars and contentions. Win them to peace by your peaceable examples.

So, also shall you be an encouragement to many of your Christian

*friends in your native country, to come to you when they hear of your Peace,
Love and Kindness among you. It shall be well with your souls when death
comes; you being found of Him, not in discontent but in brotherly love, and
peace.]*

Mr. Cushman returned back also with the Ship [the *Fortune*],
for so Mr. Weston and the rest had appointed him for their better
information. [With him he took to England for publication there
the Journal of the Pilgrims.]

The Fortune was laden with good clapboard as full as she
could stow, and two hogshead of beaver and other skins which they
got with a few trifling commodities.

... By Mr. Cushman's persuasion and letters received from
Leyden wherein they willed them so to do, the [the Pilgrims] yielded
to the aforesaid conditions and subscribed them with their hands.

Mr. Weston (as before noted) had made that large promise
in his letter that if all the rest should fall off, yet, he would never
quit the business but stick to them, if they yielded to the conditions, and sent some lading in the ship ... But all proved wind, for
he was the first and only man that forsook them.

[In a letter replying to Weston blaming Carver and the
Pilgrims, Bradford writes,] *for his [John Carver's] care and pains were
so great for the common good, both ours and yours, as that, there with, it
is thought he oppressed himself and shortened his days, of whose loss we
cannot sufficiently complain.*

*At great charges in this adventure, I confess you have been, and
many losses may sustain; but the loss of his and many other honest men's
lives cannot be valued at any price. Of the one there may be hope of recovery;
but the other no recompense can make good.*

... After the departure of this Ship which stayed not above
fourteen days, the Governor and his assistant, having disposed these
latecomers into several families, as best they could, took an exact
account of all their provisions in store and proportioned the same
to the number of persons, and found that it would not hold out above
six months at half allowance ... but they bore it patiently under hope
of supply.

Narragansett Challenge

Soon after this Ship's departure, that great people of the Narragansetts, in a braving manner, sent a messenger unto them with a bundle of arrows, tied about with a great snakeskin, which their interpreters told them was a threatening and a challenge.

Upon which the Governor, with the advice of others, sent them a round answer that if they had rather have war than peace, they might begin when they would; they had done them no wrong, neither did they fear them or should they find them unprovided. And by another messenger sent the snakeskin back with bullets in it. But they would not receive it, but sent it back again. But these things I do but mention, because they are more at large, already put forth in print by Mr. Winslow at the request of some friends [In *Good News from New England*, published in London, 1624] ... It was their ambition to domineer ... and they conceived the English to be a bar in their way, and saw that Massasoit took shelter already under their wings.

But this made them [the Pilgrims] the more carefully to look to themselves, so as they agreed to enclose their dwellings with a good strong pale, and make flankers in convenient places with gates to shut, which were every night locked, and a watch kept ... And the company was by the Captain's and the Governor's advice divided into four squadrons; and everyone had their quarter appointed them unto which they were to repair upon any sudden alarm ... And the town was impaled around by the beginning of March, in which every family had a pretty garden plot secured.

Keeping Christmas

Herein, I shall end this year. On the day called Christmas Day, the Governor called them out to work as was used. But most of the new company excused themselves and said it went against their consciences to work on that day. So the Governor told them that if they made it a matter of conscience, he would spare them till they were better informed; so he led away the rest and left them. But when they came home at noon from their work, he found them in the street at play, openly; some pitching the bar, and some at stool-ball and such sports. So he went to them and took away their implements and told them that was against his conscience, that they should play and others work.

If they made the keeping of Christmas a matter of devotion, let them keep to their houses; but there should be no gaming or reveling in the streets. Since which time, nothing hath been attempted that way.

XIII Weston's Plantation

William Bradford - Anno Domini 1622

Now in a manner, their provisions were wholly spent, and they looked hard for supply, but none came. But about the latter end of May, they spied a boat at sea, but it proved to be a shallop which came from a ship [the *Sparrow*], which Mr. Weston ... had set out afishing, forty leagues to the eastward of them.

... This boat had brought seven passengers, and some letters but no victuals, nor any hope of any.

A letter written on January 12, 1622 by Mr. Weston to Mr. John Carver says:

We daily expect the Ship (the Fortune) back again. She departed hence, the beginning of July with 35 persons, though not over-well provided with necessities, by reason of the parsimony of the Adventures. I solicited them to send you a supply of men and provisions before she came but **they all answered they will do great matters when they hear good news, nothing before.** *So faithful, constant, and careful of your good are your old and constant friends, that if they hear not from you, they are like to send you no supply.*

... Mr. John Beauchamp and myself bought this little ship; and have set her out, partly, if it may be, to uphold the Plantation, as well as to do others good as ourselves, and partly, to get up what we are formerly out, though we are otherwise censured, etc.

... We have sent this ship and these passengers on our account. We desire you will friendly entertain and supply with such necessaries as you can spare. (Also) we pray you lend or sell them some seed corn and ... that you will let them have salt for their present use.

... We intend, if God please, and the Generality do it not -,

to send within a month another ship who, having discharged her passengers shall go to Virginia. And it may be, we shall send a small ship to abide with you on the coast, which I conceive may be a great help to the Plantation.

... Some of the Adventurers have sent you, herewithal, some directions for your furtherance in the common business.

... I find the general so backward, and your friends at Leyden so cold that I fear you must stand on your legs and trust, as they say, to God and yourselves.

... All this was but cold comfort to fill their hungry bellies.

... They never had any supply of victuals more afterwards, but what the Lord gave them, otherwise, for all [that] the company sent at any time was always too short for those people that came with it.

... There came another letter by the same ship to their late Governor, Mr. Carver, from Mr. Weston:

*... The greater part of the Adventurers, being willing to uphold the business, finding it no reason that those that are willing should uphold the business of those that are unwilling ... having well considered and thereof, **having resolved**, according to an article in the agreement (that it may be lawful by a general consent of the Adventurers and Planters to break off their joint stock) thus **to break it off**; and do pray you ratify, and confirm the same on your parts. **Which being done,** we shall the more willingly go forward for the upholding of you with all things necessary. But in any case you must agree to the articles, and send it by the first under your hands and seal. So I end.*

Another letter was written from part of the company of Adventurers to the same purpose, and subscribed with nine of their names. These things seemed strange unto them, seeing inconstancy; it made them think there was some mystery in the matter. Therefore, the governor concealed these letters from the public, only imparted them to some trusty friends.

... After this came another of Weston's ships [the *Charity*, 100 tons, accompanied by the *Swan*, 30 tons]and brought letters dated the 10th of April from Mr. Weston.

To Mr. Bradford:

The Fortune is arrived, of whose good news touching your estate and proceedings I am very glad to hear. Howsoever, the Fortune was robbed on the way by the Frenchmen, yet I hope your loss will not be great.

So great a return doth animate the Adventurers, so I hope some matter of importance will be done by them.

... As for myself, I have sold my adventure and debts unto them, so I am quit of you and you of me ... I will advise you a little for your good ... I perceive and know as well as another the dispositions of your Adventurers whom the hope of gain have drawn on to this which they have done; yet I fear that hope will not draw them much farther. Besides, most of them are against the sending of them of Leyden, for whose cause this business was first begun. So that my advice is that you forewith break off your joint stock, which you have warrent to do, both in law and conscience.

The means you have there ... may with the help of some friends here bear the charge of transporting those of Leyden. And when they are with you, I make no question but by God's help you will be able to subsist of yourselves; but I leave you to your discretion.

Another letter to Mr. Bradford and Mr. Brewster from Adventurers Edward Pickering and William Greene, was intercepted by Weston, wondering what mystery might be in it:

The company bought out Mr. Weston, and are very glad they are freed of him, he being judged a man that thought himself above the General, and not expressing so much the fear of God, as was meet in a man to whom such trust should have be reposed, in a matter of so great importance.

... For by credible testimony, we are informed his purpose is to come to your colony, pretending he comes for and from the Adventurers and will seek to get what you have in readiness into his ships, as if they came from the Company's and possessing all, will be so much profit to himself.

... I am sorry that there is cause to admonish you of these things concerning this man. So I leave you to God, who bless and multiply you into the thousands.

I pray conceal both the writing and delivery of this letter, but make the best use of it.

Here we have Mr. Weston's comment on the intercepted letter:

Mr. Bradford:

My end in sending the ship Sparrow was your good ... Now I will not deny but there are many of our people, rude fellows ... yet I presume, they will be governed by such as I set over them, and I hope not only to be able to reclaim them from profaneness that may scandalize the voyage, but by degrees to draw them to God. I have charged the master of the ship, Sparrow, not only to leave with you 2000 of bread, but also a good quantity of fish. I shall leave in the country a little ship - if God send her safe thither - with mariners and fishermen to stay there, that shall coast and trade with the savages and the old Plantation.

... All his promised help turned into an empty advice, which they apprehended was neither lawful or profitable for them to follow.

They well saw Mr. Weston pursued his own ends, and was embittered in spirit.

The Governor [also] received a letter from Mr. Cushman [who went home in the *Fortune*] and was always intimate with Mr. Weston. It follows:

By God's Providence, we got well home, the 17th of February, being robbed by the Frenchmen on the way, and carried by them into France [where] we were kept 15 days. We lost all that was worth taking; but thanks be to God, we escaped with our lives and Ship.

*... **I pray you be advertised a little** [expressing desire to have published the Journal of the Pilgrims which he took to England with him on the Fortune].*

*Mr. Weston has quite broken off from our company, and sold his adventures. And hath now sent three ships for his particular plantation ... **the people which they carry are no men for us.** Wherefore, I pray you entertain them not, neither exchange man for man with them, except it be some of your worst ... **I fear these people will hardly deal so well with the savages, as they should.** I pray you signify to Squanto that they are a distinct body from us, and we have nothing to do with them.*

... Our friends at Leyden are well, and will come to you as many as can this time. Wherefore, I pray you be not discouraged, but gather up yourself to go through these difficulties cheerfully, and with courage.

... All these things they pondered; yet concluded to give his men [Mr. Weston's] friendly entertainment ... partly, in compassion to the people who were now come into a wilderness, as they themselves were.

... As they had received his former company of seven men [from the *Sparrow*] and victualized them as their own, hither to, so they, also, received these from the Charity - being about 60 lusty men -, and gave housing for them, and their goods. They stayed the most part of the summer. Then by his [Weston's] direction, or those whom he set over them, they removed to Massachusetts Bay, he having got a patent for some part there. Yet they left [with the Pilgrims] all their sick folk, till they were settled and housed, but of their victuals they had not any, though they were in great want; neither did they desire it, for **they saw that they were an unruly company, and had no good government over them.**

... When famine began to pinch them sore, they not knowing what to do, the Lord present them with an occasion beyond all expectations; a boat brought them a letter from a stranger, being a captain of a ship come there a-fishing. It follows:

Friends, Countrymen and Neighbours:

... I will so far inform you that the South colony of Virginia have received such a blow that 400 persons will not make good our losses [An Indian massacre occurred].

... Happy is he whom other men's harms doth make to beware.

Yours,

Captain Huddleston of

the Bona Nova

...This summer they built a fort with good timber, both strong and comely, which was of good defense, made with a flat roof and battlements, on which their ordnance were mounted, and where they kept constant watch, especially in time of danger. **It served them also, for a meeting house,** and was fitted accordingly for that use. It was a great work for them in this weakness and time of wants, but the danger of the time required it; and both the continual rumors of the fears from the Indians here, especially, the Narragansetts and also, hearing of that great massacre in Virginia, made all hands willing to dispatch the same.

[In Winslow's *Good News* pp. 13, 39-40, he states that the fort was begun in June 1622, and that it required ten months to complete. The work proving *"tedious"* some *"would have dissuaded from proceeding, flattering themselves with peace and security, and accounting it rather a work of superfluity, and vain-glory, than of simple necessity. The devil,"* he observes, *"will cause reasonable men to reason against their own safety."*]

Now the welcome harvest time came; in which all had hungry bellies filled. But it rose to a little in comparison to a full year's supply; partly, because they were not yet well acquainted with the manner of Indian corn, also their many other employments; but chiefly, their weakness for want of food.

... So it well appeared that famine must still ensue, the next year, also, if not some way prevented.

Behold, now, another providence of God. A ship [the *Discovery*, 60 tons] comes into the harbor one Captian Jones, being chief therein. They were set out by some merchants to discover all the harbors between this and Virginia, ... and to trade along the coast.

But I will here take liberty to make a little digression. There was in this Ship a gentleman by the name, Mr. John Pory, who had been Secretary of Virginia, and was now going home, a passenger in this ship. [He was an alumnus Caius College, Cambridge - his account of his visit to Plymouth was recently discovered and published in 1917 for the first time, and is in possession of Brown University Library. The manuscript in letter form gives a glowing story of Plymouth Plantation which would have filled the hearts of the Pilgrims with pride.]

[Pory relates: *After some dangerous and almost inconceivable errors and mistakings, he [Pilot of **Mayflower**] stumbled by accident upon the harbour of Plymouth, where after the Planters had failed of their intention and the pilot of his, it pleased Almighty God [who had better provided for them than their own hearts could imagine] to plant them on the site of an old town [Patuxet] which divers years before had been abandoned by the Indians. So they both quietly and justly sat down without either dispossessing any of the natives or being resisted by them even ... who generally do acknowledge not only the seat ... but do themselves disclaim all title from it, so the right of the Planters to it is altogether of a favour.*

... To describe the excellence of the place, first, the harbor is not only pleasant air, but also prospect most sure for shipping both small and great, being land-locked on all sides. The town is seated on the ascent of a hill ... such is the wholesomeness of the place, as Governor Bradford told me, that for the pace of one whole year of the two wherein they had been there, died not one man, woman or child. This healthfulness is accompanied with much plenty, both of fish and fowl...

The reasons of their continued plenty for those 7 months in the year may be the continual tranquility of the place, being guarded on all sides by the fury of the storms, also, the abundance of food they find at low water ... and lastly, the number of friskels [brooks] running into the bay where they may refresh and quench their thirst.

Now concerning the quality of the people, how happy were it for our people in the Southern colony [Virginia] if they were as free from wickedness and vice, as these are in this place. And their industry as well appeareth by their people as by [who built] a substantial palisade about their settlement of 2700 foot in compass, stronger than I have seen in Virginia, and lastly, by a blockhouse, which they have erected in the highest place of the town to mount their ordnance upon, from whence they command all the harbor ... As touching their correspondence with the Indians, they are friends with all their neighbors."]

Shortly, after harvest Mr. Weston's people who were now seated at the Massachusetts Bay, and by disorder, - as it seems -, had made havoc of their provisions, began now to perceive that want would come upon them. And hearing that they here had bought trading commodities, and intended to trade for corn, they writ to the Governor and desired they might join with them, and they would employ their small ship in the service, and further, requested either to lend or sell them so much of their trading commodities as their part might come to, and they would undertake to make payment when ... their supply should come. The Governor condescended upon equal terms of agreement, thinking to go about the Cape to the southward with the ship where some store of corn might be got.

... Captain Standish was appointed to go with them and Squanto for a guide and interpreter about the latter end of September, but their winds put them into again; and pulling out the second time, Standish fell ill of a fever so the Governor went himself. But they could not get about the shoals of Cape Cod, so they put into Manamoyick Bay. In this place Squanto fell sick of an Indian fever, bleeding much at the nose and within a few days died there; desiring the Governor to pray for him that he might go the Englishmen's God in Heaven.

They got in this voyage in one place about 26 or 28 hogsheads of corn and beans; which was more than the Indian could well spare in these parts.

... In February a messenger came from John Sanders, chief over Mr. Weston's men in the Bay of Massachusetts, who brought a letter showing the great wants they were fallen into; and he would have borrowed a hogshead of corn of the Indians, but they would lend him none. He desired advice whether he might not take it from them by force to succour his men till he came from the eastward whither he was going. **The Governor and rest dissuaded him by all means from it, for it would so exasperate the Indians as it might endanger their safety,** and all of us might smart for it; for they had already heard how they had so wronged the Indians by stealing their corn.

Yea, so base were some of their own company, as they went and told the Indians that their Governor was purposed to come and take their corn by force, the which, with other things made them enter into a conspiracy against the English.

XIV Sad straits of Weston's men, and the great Indian conspiracy

William Bradford - Anno Domini 1623

It may be thought strange that these people should fall to these extremities in so short a time; being left completely provided when the ship left them ... **It must needs be their great disorder, for they spent excessively whilst they had or could get it.**

... Whilst things went in this manner with them, the Governor and people here had notice that Massasoit, their friend, was sick and near unto death. They sent [some of their men] to visit him, and withal [took] him such comfortable things as gave him great content, and was a means of his recovery. Upon which occasion, **he [Massasoit] discovers the conspiracy of these Indians, how they were resolved to cut off Mr. Weston's people for the continual injuries they did them**, and would now take opportunity of their weakness to do it, and for that end had conspired with other Indians, their neighbors, thereabout, ... and solicited him [Massasoit] to join with them. He advised them, therefore, to prevent it, and that speedily ... for he assured them of the truth hereof. This did much trouble them, and they took it into serious deliberation, and found upon examination, other evidence to [give] light, hereunto.

In the meantime, came one of them from Massachusetts Bay [Phineas Pratt, who became later the sole survivor of the Weston colony] with a small pack at his back, and though he knew not a foot of the way, yet he got safe hither, having lost his way which was well for him, for he was pursued, and so was missed. He told them how all things stood amongst them, and that he must durst stay no longer; he apprehended that they [Weston's men] by what he observed would all be knocked in the head shortly.

... This made them make the more haste, and they dispatched a boat away with Captain Standish and some men, who found them in a miserable condition out of which he rescued them and helped them to some relief. They thanked him and the rest, but most of them desired to go with their small ship to the eastward where happily they might hear of Mr. Weston or some supply from him, seeing the time of the year was for fishing ships to be in the land; if not, they would work among the fishermen for their living, and get their passage to England, if they heard nothing from Mr. Weston.

... **This was the end of these, that sometime boasted of their strength and what they would do and bring to pass in comparison of the people here,** who had many women and children and weak ones amongst them. And said at their first arrival, when they saw the wants here that they would take another course, and not to fall into such a condition as this simple people were to come. But a man's way is not in his own power; God can make the weak to stand. Let him also that standeth take heed, lest he fall.

Shortly after, Mr. Weston came over with some of the fishermen, under another name, and in the disguise of a blacksmith where he heard of the ruin and dissolution of his colony. He got a boat and with a man or two came to see how things were. But along the way, for want of skill, in a storm he cast away his Shallop in the bottom of the Bay and hardly escaped with his life. Afterwards, he fell into the hands of the Indians who pillaged him.

He finally got means to come to Plymouth. A strange alteration there was in him, to such as had seen and known him in his former flourishing condition ... After much discourse, he desired to borrow some beaver of them; and told them he had hope of a ship and good supply to come to him, and then they should have anything they stood in need of ... They had not much beaver and if they should let him have it, it were enough to make a mutiny among the people, seeing there was no other means to procure them food. Yet they told him they would help him considering his necessity. So they let him have 100 beaver skins. **Thus, they helped him when all the world failed him,** and with this means he went again to the Ships ... But he requited them ill, he proved after a bitter enemy unto them upon all occasions and never repaid them for anything for it to this day, but reproaches and evil words.

End of Common Planting;
Land apportionment by Families

... All this while no supply was heard of, neither knew they when they might expect any. So they began to think how they might raise as much corn as they could, and obtain a better crop than they had done, that they might not still, thus, lanquish in misery. At length, after much debate of things, with the advice of the chiefest amongst them, they gave way that **they should set corn every man for his own particular, and in that regard trust to themselves;** but in all other things to go on in the general way as before.

... And so was assigned to every man a parcel of land, according to the proportion of their number for that end, only for present use - no division being made for inheritance - and ranged all boys and youth under some family. This had very good success for it made all hands very industrious, so as much more corn was planted than otherwise would have been by any other means; and saved a great deal of trouble and gave far better content. The women now went willingly into the field, and took their little ones with them to set corn; which before would allege weakness and inability; whom to have compelled would have been thought great tyranny and oppression.

The experience that was had in this common course and condition tried several years [1620-1623] and that among godly and sober men, may well evince the vanity of that conceit of Plato's ... that the taking away of property and bringing into community ... would make them happy and flourishing; as if they were wiser than God.

... But they deemed it a kind of slavery ... God in his wisdom saw another course fitter for them.

After this course settled, and their corn was planted, all their victuals were spent, and they were only to rest on God's providence, at night, not many times knowing where to have a bit of anything the next day. **And so, as one well observed, had need to pray that God would give them their daily bread.** They having but one boat left, and she not over-well fitted, they were divided into several companies, six or seven to a gang or company and so went out, with a net they had bought to take bass and such like fish, by course, every company knowing its turn. No sooner was the boat discharged of what she brought but the next company took her and went out with her. Neither did they return till they had caught something, though it were five or six days before, for they knew that there was nothing at home, and to go home empty would be a great discouragement to the rest ... Then all went seeking of shellfish, and this was their living in summertime; and in the winter they were helped with ground nuts and fowl. Also in the summer, they got now and then a deer.

... In June, 1623, came the Ship called the *Anne*, whereof Mr. William Peirce was the master. They brought about 60 persons for the General [including George Morton who was publisher of the *Journal of the Pilgrims* in 1622, and his son Nathaniel, then 12 years old, who later became Secretary of the Colony, and wrote *New England's Memorial* in 1669] and also 60 tons of goods. Some of them being very useful persons and became good members of the body; and some were the wives and children of such as were here already. And some were so bad as they were fain to be at charge to send them home the next year.

Also, besides these there came a company that did not belong to the General Body but came on their own Particular, and were to have lands assigned them and be for themselves, yet to be subject to the general government; which caused some difference and disturbance amongst them, as will after appear.

In a letter from Robert Cushman, he says:

...Neither indeed have we now sent you many things which we should and would, for want of money ... I pray you write earnestly to the

Treasurer, and direct what persons should be sent. It grieveth me to see so weak a company sent you, and yet had I not been here, they had been weaker. You must still call upon the company here to see that honest men be sent you,

And from the General comes the following letter:

... We have in this Ship sent such women as were willing and ready to go to their husbands and friends with their children. We would not have you discontented because we have not sent you more of your old friends, and especially him on whom you most depend (John Robinson).

... There are, also, come unto you some honest men to plant upon their own Particulars beside you, a thing which if we should not give way unto, we should wrong both them and you; them by putting them on things more inconvenient; and you, for that their being honest men, they will be a strengthening to the place and good neighbours unto you.

... Two things we would advise you of; first, the trade for skins to be retained for the General till the dividend; secondly, that their settling by you be with such distance of place as is neither inconvenient for the lying of your lands, nor hurtful to your speedy and easy assembling together.

We have sent you divers fishermen with salt. Divers other provisions we have sent you, as will appear in your bill of lading and though we have not sent all we would yet it is as we could.

And although it seemeth, you have discovered many more rivers and fertile grounds than where you are; yet seeing by God's providence, that place fell to your lot, let it be accounted as your portion, and rather fix your eyes upon that which may be done there than languish in hopes after things elsewhere. If your place be not the best, it is the better; you shall be less envied and encroached upon; and such as are earthly minded will not settle too near your border. If the land afford you bread, and the sea yield you fish, rest you awhile contented; God will one day afford you better fare. And all men shall know you are neither fugitives nor discontents, but can, if God so order it, take the worst to yourselves with content, and leave the best too your neighbours with cheerfulness.

Let it not be grievous unto you that you have been instruments to break the ice for others who come after with less difficulty; the honor shall be yours to the world's end.

*And so the Lord be with you and all, and send us **joyful news** from you.*

... These passengers of the *Anne* when they saw their low and poor condition ashore, were much daunted and dismayed ... Some wished themselves in England again; others fell aweeping, fancying their own misery in what they saw now in others; some pitying the distress they saw in their friends which they had been long in, and still were under. In a word, all were full of sadness. Only some of their old friends rejoiced to see them, and that it was no worse with them, for they could not expect it should be better, and now hoped they should enjoy better days together.

... But God fed them out of the sea for the most part.

A great drought continued from the third week in May, till about the middle of July, without any rain and with great heat, in-so-much as the corn began to wither away, though it was set with fish.

Upon which they set apart a solemn day of humiliation, to seek the Lord by humble and fervent prayer in this great distress.

He was pleased to give them a gracious and speedy answer, both to their own, and the Indians admiration that lived amongst them. For all that morning, and greatest part of the day, it was clear weather and very hot, and not a cloud or any sign of rain to be seen; yet toward evening it began to overcast and shortly after to rain with such sweet and gentle showers, as gave them cause of rejoicing and blessing God. It came without wind or thunder or any violence. Which did so apparently revive and quicken the decayed corn and other fruits, as was wonderful to see. Through His blessing was caused a fruitful and liberal harvest to their no small comfort and rejoicing.

For which mercy in time convenient, they also set apart a day of Thanksgiving [Bradford issued a proclamation saying - Through virtue of vested power - ye shall gather with one accord, and hold, in the month of November, Thanksgiving unto the Lord. A custom made into law November 15, 1636 - Plymouth Col. Rec. XI 18].

... The Old Planters were afraid that their corn when it was ripe should be imparted to the Newcomers.

... Let the Newcomers enjoy what they had brought; the Pilgrims would have none of it, except they could purchase any of it of them by bargain or exchange. **It gave both sides good content;** for the Newcomers were as much afraid that the hungry Planters would have eaten up the provisions brought, and they should have fallen into the like condition.

The ship was in a short time laden with clapboard by the

help of many hands. Also, they sent in her all the beaver and other furs they had. **And Mr. Edward Winslow was sent over with her to inform of all things and procure such things as were thought needful for their present condition.**

By this time harvest was come, and instead of famine now, God gave them plenty, and the face of things was changed. Any general want or famine hath not been amongst them since this day.

Those that came over on their Particular looked for greater matters than they found, or could attain unto, about building great houses, and such pleasant situations for them as themselves had fancied, as if they would be great men and rich men all of a sudden. But they proved castles in the air. Herewith are the conditions agreed on between the Colony and them:

1. That the Governor in the name and with the consent of the Company, doth in love and friendship receive and embrace them, and is to allot them competent places for habitations within the town.

2. That they on their parts be subject to all such laws and orders as are already made, or hereafter, shall be for the public good.

3. That they be freed and exempt from general employments of said company which their present condition of community requireth, except common defense, and such other employments, as tend to the perpetual good of the Colony.

4. Towards the maintenance of government, and public affairs every male above the age of sixteen years shall pay a bushel of Indian wheat or worth of it into the common store.

5. That according to the agreement the merchants made with them before they came, they are to be debarred from all trade with the Indians, for all sorts of furs and such like commodities, till the time of the communality be ended.

... About the middle of September arrived Captain Robert Gorges in the bay of Massachusetts with sundry passengers and families, intending there to begin a plantation; and pitched upon the place Mr. Weston's people had foresaken. He had a commission from the Council of New England to be general governor of the country. [Gorges and his passengers were kindly entertained at Plymouth - and stayed two weeks - then they were piloted by the Pilgrims to the new plantation.]

The Ship then fitted herself to go for Virginia, having some passengers there to deliver. And with her returned sundry of those hence which came over on their particular, some out of discontent and dislike of the country. Others by reason of a fire that broke out and burned the houses they lived in, and all their provisions.

... The house in which the fire began was right against their storehouse, which they had much ado to save ... if it had been lost the plantation would have been overthrown. But through God's mercy, it was saved by the great diligence of the people.

... Some would have had the goods thrown out; but if they had, there would have been much stolen by the rude company that belonged to these two ships ... But a trusty company was placed within; as well as those that with wet cloths kept off the fire.

... They suspected some malicious dealing, if not plain treachery, and whether it was only suspicion or not, God knows; but this is certain, when the tumult was greatest, **there was a voice heard** — but from whom it was not known — **that bid them look well about them for all were not friends that were near them.** And shortly after, when the vehemency of the fire was over, smoke was seen to rise within the shed that was joined to the end of the storehouse. ... Some running to quench [the fire] found a long firebrand of an eel long, lying under the wall on the inside, which could not possibly come there by casualty but must be laid there by some hand.

But God Kept them from this danger, whatever was intended.

XV   Changes in election of officers; Coming of Cattle, etc.

William Bradford - Anno Domini 1624

The time of new election of their officers being come, and the number of their people increased, and their troubles therewith, the Governor desired them to change the persons ... and also to add more Assistants to the Governor for help and counsel, and the better carrying on of affairs ... The issue was that, as before there was but one Assistant, they now chose five, giving the Governor a double voice; and afterwards they increased them to seven.

... Shortly after Mr. Edward Winslow [who had returned to England on the *Anne*] came over [on the *Charity*] and brought a good supply ... He brought three heifers and a bull, the first beginning of any cattle of that kind in the land, with some clothing and other necessaries.

... I must also speak a word of the planting of the Particulars this year. They, having found the benefit of their last years harvest, and setting corn for their Particular, having thereby with a great deal of patience, overcome hunger and famine. Which makes me remember a saying of Seneca's Epistle 123: **"That a great part of liberty is a well-governed belly, and to be patient in all wants."**

They began now to prize corn as more precious than silver, and those that had some to spare began to trade one with another for small things by the quart, pottle [2 quarts] and pecks; for money they had none, and if they had, corn was preferred before it. That they might increase their tillage to better advantage; they made suit to the Governor to have some portion of the land given them for continuance, and not be yearly lot.

103

... Which being well considered, their request was granted. And to every person was given only one acre of land, to them and theirs, as near the town as might be; and they had no more till the seven years expired. The reason was that they might be kept close together, both for more safety and defense, and the better improvement of the general employments.

... The ship-carpenter that was sent over was an honest and very industrious man, and followed his labour very diligently, and made all that were employed with him do the like. He quickly built them two very good, and strong shallops, which after did them great service.

... But he whom they sent to make salt was an ignorant, foolish, self-willed fellow ... For he could not do anything but boil salt in pans, and yet would make them that were joined with him, believe there was so great a mystery in it as was not easy to be attained, and made them do many unnecessary things to blind their eyes, till they discerned his subtlety.

... The third eminent person they [the Adventurers] sent over which was the minister by name of Mr. John Lyford, of whom and whose doing I must be more large. When this man first came ashore, he saluted them with that reverence and humility as is seldom to be seen ... He bowed and cringed; yea, he wept, blessing God that had brought him to see their faces, and admiring things they had done in their wants. Yet all the while - if we may judge by his after carriages -, he was like him mentioned in Psalm X:10 "That croucheth and boweth, so that heaps of poor may fall by his might".

... They gave him the best entertainment they could, in all simplicity, and a larger allowance of food out of the store than any other had; and as the Governor had used, in all weighty affairs to consult with their Elder, Mr. Brewster, together with his Assistants, so now he called Mr. Lyford also, to counsel with them in their weightiest businesses.

After some short time, he desired to join himself a member of the church here, and was accordingly received. He made a large confession of his faith, and an acknowledgement of his former disorderly walking, and his being entangled with many corruptions, which had been a burden to his conscience, and blessed God for this opportunity of freedom and liberty, to enjoy the ordinances of God in purity among His people.

I must speak here a word also, of Mr. John Oldham who was a copartner with him in his after courses. He had been a chief stickler in the former faction among the Particulars, and an intelligencer to those in England. But now, since the coming of this ship, the Charity, and he saw the supply that came, he took occasion to open his mind to some of the chief amongst them here, and confessed he had done them wrong both by word and deed. **But now he saw the eminent hand of God to be with them, and His blessing upon them,** which made his heart smite him; neither should those in England ever use him as an instrument any longer against them in anything. He also desired former things might be forgotten.

...Thus all things seemed to go very comfortably and smoothly on amongst them, at which they did much rejoice. But this lasted not long, for both Oldham and Lyford grew worse, and showed a spirit of great malignancy, drawing many into faction as they could ... So as there was nothing but private meetings and whisperings amongst them; they feeding themselves and others with what they should bring to pass in England by the faction of their friends there, which brought others as well as themselves into a fool's paradise.

... At length when the Ship was ready to go [the *Charity* to return to England] it was observed that Lyford was long in writing and sent many letters, and could not forbear to communicate to his intimates such things, as made them laugh in their sleeves; and thought he had done their errand sufficiently. The Governor and some other of his friends, knowing how things stood in England, and what hurt these things might do, took a Shallop and went out with the Ship a league or two to sea, and called for all Lyford's and Oldham's letters. Mr. William Peirce being Master of the Ship, and knew well their evil dealing both in England and here, afforded him all the assistance he could. He found above twenty of Lyford's letters, many of them large and full of slanders and false accusations, tending not only to their prejudice, but to their ruin and utter subversion.

... This Ship went out towards evening and in the night the Governor returned. [It was thought] that the Governor went but to dispatch his own letters. The reason why the Governor and rest concealed these things the longer was to let things ripen, that they might better discover their intents and see who were their adherents. And the rather because amongst the rest they found a letter of one of the confederates, in which was written that Mr. Oldham and Mr. Lyford intended a reformation in the church and commonwealth, as soon as the Ship was gone.

For Oldham, few of his letters were found, for he was so bad a scribe as his hand was scarce legible, yet he was in as deep in mischief as the other. And thinking they were now strong enough, they began to pick quarrels at everything.

... But to cut things short, at length it grew to this issue, that Lyford with his complices, without ever speaking one word either to the Governor, Church or Elder, withdrew themselves and set up a public meeting apart of the Lord's Day; with sundry such insolent carriages, too long here to relate, beginning now publicly to act what privately they had been long plotting.

It was now thought high time, to prevent further mischief, to call them to account. So the Governor called a court, and summoned the whole company to appear. And then charged Lyford and Oldham with such things as they were guilty of. They stood resolutely upon the denial of most things and required proof.

... The Governor produced ... the letters [written] under his own hand [and Oldham's, too] and caused them to be read before all the people, at which [their] friends were blank and had not a word to say.

[The Pilgrims] alleged [that by] what was writ to them out of England, it was evident they joined in plotting against them and disturbing their peace, both in respect to their civil and church state.

... But they and all the world knew, they came hither to enjoy the liberty of their conscience, and the free use of God's ordinances, and for that end had ventured their lives, and passed through so much hardship hitherto; and they and their friends had borne the charge of these beginning which was not small. And that Lyford for his part was sent over on this charge and that both he and his great family were maintained on the same, and also was joined to the church and a member of them. And for him to plot against them, and seek their ruin was most unjust and perfidious.

... In conclusion, he was fully convicted and burst out into tears, and confessed he was a reprobate, and that he had so wronged them that they could never make amends. After their trial, the court censured them to be expelled from the place. Oldham presently, though his wife and family had liberty to stay all winter. Lyford had liberty to stay six months.

In Exile, Lyford wrote, "I do freely confess I dealt very indiscretely in some of my particular letters I wrote to private friends ... but I am heartily sorry for it, and do to the glory of God, and mine own shame acknowledge it."

[It is surmised that part of the reason that Lyford was sent by the Adventurers was to keep back John Robinson, and some others from Leyden from coming, as is indicated in letters from the Leyden pastor, "or all will be spoiled."]

Robinson wrote to Bradford: *Our love and care, too, for you is mutual, though our hopes of coming unto you be small and weaker than ever.*

.. The Adventurers, it seems, have neither money nor any great mind of us, for the most part. They deny it to be any part of the covenants betwixt us that they should transport us, neither do I look for any further help from them, till means come from you.

And to Mr. Brewster, Robinson writes: And I persuade myself that, for me, they of all others are unwilling I should be transported, especially such of them as have an eye that way themselves, as thinking if I come there, their market will be marred in many regards.

... A notable experiment of this they gave in your messenger's [Winslow] presence, constraining the company to promise that none of the money now gathered should be expended or employed to the help of any towards you.

[*James Sherley, treasurer of the Adventurers wrote: We have some amongst us which undoubtedly aim more at their own private ends and the thwarting and opposing of some here, and other worthy instruments of God's glory elsewhere, than at the general good, and furtherance of this noble and laudable action.*

Robert Cushman wrote of Lyford: The preacher we have sent [we hope] is an honest and plain man, though none of the most eminent and rare. About choosing him into office, use your own liberty and discretion; he knows he is no officer amongst you, though perhaps custom and universality may make him forget himself. Mr Winslow and myself gave way to his going to give content here, and we see no hurt in it, but only his great charge of children.]

PILGRIM MAIDEN: A study of statue in Brewster Garden at Plymouth by Frank Hockaday.

XVI Oldham repents; the Company of Adventurers breaks up. Standish goes to London

William Bradford - Anno Domini 1625

Though it was part of Oldham's censure not to return without leave first obtained, yet in his daring spirit, he came back. And not only so, but suffered his unruly passion to run beyond the limits of all reason and modesty. Mr William Peirce and Mr. Edward Winslow who had just returned from England on the Charity bade them not spare Oldham for they [he and Lyford] had played the villains with them. So he was committed until he was tamer.

... But that I may make an end with him, I shall here once for all relate what befell him... After the removal of his family, ... he intended a voyage for Virginia. But it so pleased God that the bark that carried him ... was in danger [near the shoals] as they [he and other passengers] despaired of life; so he fell to prayer, and began to examine his conscience and to confess his sins, as did most burden him ... And Mr. Oldham did make a large confession of the wrongs and hurt he had done to the people and church here ... as that he had sought their ruin, so that God now met with him and might destroy him. He prayed God to forgive him and made vows that if the Lord spared his life he would become otherwise ... It pleased God to spare their lives [he with his family], though they lost their voyage; and in time afterwards, Oldham carried himself fairly towards them [the Pilgrims], and had liberty to go and come and converse with them at his pleasure, he and his family later going to the Bay of Massachusetts where he was killed by some Indians.

... This storm being blown over, yet sundry sad effects followed the same; for the Company of Adventurers broke in pieces, and the greatest part wholly deserted the Colony in regard of any further supply or care of their subsistence.

... But I shall return to the rest of their friends that stuck with them and I shall insert part of a letter herewith that came on the Charity.

To our loving friends:

Though the thing we feared be come upon us, yet we cannot forget you.

... The former course, for the Generality is wholly dissolved from what it was, and whereas, you and we, were formerly sharers and partners in all voyages and dealings, this way is now no more, but you and we are left to bethink what course to take in the future, that your lives and our moneys be not lost.

... Now we think it but reason that all such things, as there appertain to the General, be kept and preserved together and rather increased daily than any way be dispersed or embezzled away for any private ends or intents whatsoever. And after your necessities are served, you gather together such commodities as the country yields, and send them over to pay debts and clear engagement here, which are not less than L1400. And we hope you will do your best to free our engagements. Let us all endeavor to keep a free and honest course. We still are persuaded you are the people that must make a Plantation in those remote places, when all others fail and return.

... And lastly, be you entreated to walk circumspectly, and carry yourselves so uprightly in all your ways, as that no man may make just exceptions against you. And more especially, that the favour and countenance of God may be so toward you as that you may find abundant joy and peace even amidst tribulations.

... We have sent you here some cattle, cloth, hose, shoes, leather, etc; but in another nature than formerly [the Planters were to pay in goods and money,] ... Go on, good friends, comfortably; pluck up your spirits and quit yourselves like men in all your difficulties ... that the work may go on you are about, and not be neglected; which is so much for the glory of God.

The Company, which still clave to them [the settlers] sent over also two ships on fishing on their own account. The one was a pinnace that was cast away the last year here in the country and recovered by the Planters [this was the *Little James*]; which, after she came home, was attached by one of the Company for his particular debt and now sent again on this account.

The other was a great ship [*White Angel*] which was well fitted with an experienced master and company of fishermen to make the voyage.

... The master, seeing so much goods come, put it aboard the bigger ship for more safety. But Mr. Winslow, their factor in this business, was bound in a bond of L500 to send it to London in the small ship. There was some contending between the master and him about it, so it went in the small ship and he sent bills of lading in both.

The master was so careful being so well laden as they went joyfully home together, for he towed the lesser ship at his stern all the way. They had such fair weather as he never cast her off till they were shot deep in the English channel within sight of Plymouth.

And yet there she was unhappily taken by a Turks man-of-war and carried into Salee on coast of French Morocco, where master and men were made slaves and many of the beaver skins were sold for 4 d apiece. Thus all their hopes were dashed and the joyful news they meant to carry home turned to heavy tidings.

In the bigger of these ships, the White Angel, was sent [to England] Captain Standish from the Plantation with letters and instructions to their friends of the Company and also to the Honourable Council of New England. Seeing that they meant only to let them have goods upon sale, that they might have them on easier terms, for they should never be able to bear such high interest rates.

But he came at a very bad time, for the state was full of trouble and the plague very hot in London, so as no business could be done. Yet he spake with some of the honoured council who promised all helpfulness to the Plantation. So he returned a passenger in a fishing ship, having prepared a good way for the composition that was afterward made. In the meantime it pleased the Lord to give the Plantation peace and health and contented minds, as they had corn sufficient.

XVII Captain Standish arrives home with Sad News

William Bradford - Anno Domini 1626

About the beginning of April, they heard of Captain Standish's arrival, and sent a boat to fetch him home, and the things he had brought. Welcome he was, but the news be brought was sad in many regards.

... Mr. Robinson, their pastor, was dead, which struck them with much sorrow and sadness. His and their adversaries had been long and continually plotting how they might hinder his coming hither but the Lord had appointed him a better place.

Roger White, brother-in-law of Rev. John Robinson, writes of the Leyden congregations' faithful pastor's death.

He began to be sick on Saturday in the morning, the next day, being the Lord's Day, he taught us twice. So the week after he grew weaker. He had a continual inward ague, but free from infection, so that all his friends came freely to him. And if prayers, tears or means would have saved him, he had not gone hence. But he, having faithfully finished his course, and performed his work, which the Lord had appointed him to do, he now rested with the Lord in eternal happiness.

... For other news ... we have lost our old King James ... who departed life since brother Robinson.

He [Myles Standish] further, brought them notice of the death of Robert Cushman, whom the Lord took away also this year ... who for divers years had done business with the Adventurers to their great advantage ... He had writ this year ... of his ... purpose to come over and spend his [last] days with them. It show that a man's ways are not in his own power. **Man may purpose, but God doth dispose.**

It is a marvel it did not wholly discourage them and sink them. But they gathered up their spirits ... and began to rise again.

... The Planters finding their corn to be a commodity, - for they sold it at 6 s. a bushel, used great diligence in planting the same.

... This year they sent Mr. Allerton into England and gave him order to make a composition with the Adventurers upon as good terms as he could ... But yet enjoined him not to conclude absolutely till they [the Pilgrims] knew the terms and had well considered of them, but to drive it to as good an issue as he could, and refer the conclusion to them.

XVIII New Deal with the Adventurers and within the Colony—Land Division

William Bradford - Anno Domini 1627

At the usual season of the coming of ships, Mr. Isaac Allerton returned, and brought some useful goods with him, according to the order given him. For upon his commission he took up L200 which he now got at 30%. The which goods they got safely home, and well conditioned, which was much to the comfort and content of the Plantation. He declared unto them, also, how with much ado, and no small trouble he had made a compromise with the Adventurers, by the help of sundry of their faithful friends there, who had also taken much pains thereabout. The agreement or bargain he had brought a draft of, with a list of their names thereto annexed, drawn by the best counsel of law they could get to make it firm. "... The said Isaac Allerton doth for him, his heirs, and assigns, covenant, promise and grant to and with the Adventurers, whose names are hereunto subscribed, their heirs, etc., well and truly pay or cause to be paid unto the said Adventurers or five of them which were at the meeting, aforesaid, nominated and deputed; viz. John Pocock, John Beauchamp, Robert Keane, Edward Bass and James Sherley, merchants, their heirs, etc., to and for the use of the Generality of them the sum of L1800 of lawful money of England, at the place appointed for the receipts of money, on the west side of the Royal Exchange in London; by L200 yearly, and every year on the feast of St. Michael the first payment to be made Anno 1628, etc. (subscribed November 15, 1626)"

... This agreement was very well liked of, and approved by all the Plantation, and consented unto, though they knew not how to raise the payment, and discharge their other engagements, and supply the yearly wants of the Plantation, seeing they were forced for their necessities to take up money or goods at so high interests.

Yet they undertook it, and seven or eight of the chief of the place became jointly bound for the payment of this L1800 in behalf of the rest. In which they ran a great adventure, as their present state stood, having many other heavy burdens already upon them, and all things in an uncertain condition amongst them.

... Now though they had some untoward persons mixed amongst them from the first, which came out of England [the Strangers], and more, afterwards, by some of the Adventurers, as friendship or other affections let them; ... so the Governor and Council with other of their chief friends had serious consideration how to settle things in regard of this new bargain or purchase made, in respect to the distribution of things, both for the present and future. For the present, except peace and union were preserved, they should be able to do nothing, but endanger to overthrow all, now that other ties and bonds were taken away.

Therefore, they resolved, for sundry reasons, to take in all amongst them that were either heads of families, or single young men, that were of ability and free, - and able to govern themselves with meet discretion, and their affairs, so as to be helpful in the commonwealth - into this partnership or purchase.

First, they considered that they had need of men and strength, both for defense and carrying on of business. Secondly, most of them had borne their parts in former miseries and wants with them, and therefore, in some sort should equally partake in a better condition, if the Lord pleased it. But chiefly they saw not how peace would be preserved without so doing, but danger and great disturbance might grow to their great hurt and prejudice, otherwise. Yet, they resolved to keep such a mean in distribution of lands, and other courses, as should not hinder their growth in others coming to them.

So they called the company together and conferred with them, and came to this conclusion, that the trade would be managed as before, to help pay the debts, and all such persons, as were above named, should be reputed and enrolled for purchasers; single free men to have a single share, and every father of a family to be allowed to purchase so many shares as he had persons in his family, that is to say, one for himself and one for his wife; and for every child that he had living with him, one share. As for servants, they had none but what either their masters should give them out of theirs, or their deservings should obtain from the company afterwards.

Thus, all were to be cast into single shares according to the order above said; and so every one was to pay his part according to his proportion towards the purchase, and all other debts, what the profit of the trade would not reach to: viz, a single man for a single share, a master of a family for so many as he had. **This gave good content.**

Accordingly, the few cattle which they had were divided, a cow to six persons or shares, and two goats to the same. Then **they agreed that every person or share should have 20 acres of land divided unto them**, besides the single acres they had already ... Also every share or 20 acres was to be laid out five acres in breadth by the waterside, and four acres in length.

This distribution settled men's minds. ... That they might better take all convenient opportunity to follow their trade, both to maintain themselves and to disengage them of those great sums, which they stood charged with, and bound for, they resolved to build a small pinnace at Manomet, a place 20 miles from the Plantation, standing on the sea to the Southward of them, unto which by another creek on this side, they could carry their goods within four or five miles, and then transport them overland to their vessel. And thus avoid the compassing of Cape Cod, and those dangerous shoals, and so make any voyage to the Southward in much shorter time and with far less danger. Also, for the safety of their vessel and goods, they built a house there, and kept some servants, who also planted corn and raised some swine and were always ready to go out with the bark when there was occasion. **All which took good effect, and turned to their profit.**

They now sent with the return of the ships, Mr. Allerton again into England, giving him full power under their hands and seal to conclude the former bargain with the Adventurers, and sent their bonds for the payment of the money. Also, they sent what beaver they could spare to pay some of their engagements, and to defray his charges, for those deep interest rates still kept them low. In addition he had order to procure a patent for a fit trading place in the river of Kennebec.

... Before they sent Mr. Allerton away for England this year, the Governor and some of their chief friends had serious consideration, not only how they might discharge those great engagements, which lay so heavily upon them, as is afore mentioned; but also how they might - if they possibly could - devise means to help some of their friends and brethren of Leyden over unto them, who desired so much to come to them, and they desired as much their company. To effect which, they resolved to run a high course and great adventure, not knowing, otherwise, how to bring it about. Which was to hire the trade of the company for certain years and in that time to undertake to pay that L1800 and all the rest of the debts that lay upon the Plantation, which was about L600 more; and so to set them free, and return the trade to the Generality again at the end of the term. Upon which resolution, they called the company together and made it clearly appear unto all what their debts were, and upon what terms they would undertake to pay them all in such a time, and set them clear. But their other ends, they were fain to keep secret, having only privately acquainted some of their trusty friends therewith.

... After some agitation of the thing with the company, it was yielded unto and the agreement made upon the conditions following.

"Articles of agreement between the Colony of New Plymouth of the one party, and William Bradford, Captain Myles Standish, Isaac Allerton, and such others, as they shall think good to take as partners with them, concerning the trade for beaver, and other furs and commodities. (Made July 1627):

First, it is agreed that the aforesaid have undertaken and agree to pay, discharge and acquit said Colony of all the debts both due for the purchase, or any other belonging to them at the day of the date of these presents.

Secondly, the above said parties are to have and freely enjoy the Pinnace lately built, the boat at Manomet, and the Shallop called the bass boat with all other implements to them belonging, this is, in the store of the said Company.

Thirdly, that the above said Company (parties) have the whole trade to themselves, their heirs, and assigns as the said colony doth now or may use for six full years, to begin last of September next ensuing.

Fourthly, in further consideration of the discharge of the said debts, every several purchaser doth promise, and covenant yearly to pay or cause to be payed, to the above-said parties, during the full term of six years, three bushels of corn or six pounds of tobacco, at the Undertakers' choice.

Fifthly, the said Undertakers shall during the aforesaid term bestow L50 per annum in hose and shoes, to be brought over for the Colony's use, and to be sold unto them for corn at 6S per bushel.

Sixthly, that **at the end of the said term of six years, the whole trade shall return to the use and benefit of said Colony, as before.**

Lastly, if the aforesaid Undertakers, after they have acquainted their friends in England with these covenants, do upon the first return, resolve to perform them, and undertake to discharge of the debts of said Colony, according to the true meaning and intent of these presents."

Mr. Allerton carried a copy of this agreement with him into England, and amongst other instructions had order given him to deal with some of their special friends to join them in this trade upon the above recited conditions; as also to impart their further end that moved them to take this course, namely, **the helping over of some of their friends from Leyden as they should be able, in which, if any of them would join with them, they should thankfully accept of their love and partnership herein.**

XIX   About their Debts, and Correspondence with the Undertakers

William Bradford - Anno Domini 1628

After Mr. Allerton's arrival in England, he acquainted them with his commission, and his full power to conclude the forementioned bargain and purchase. Upon the view whereof, and the delivery of the bonds for the payment of the money yearly - as is before mentioned - it was fully concluded, and a deed fairly engrossed in parchment was delivered him, under their hands and seals, confirming the same. Moreover, he dealt with them about other things according to his instruction, as to admit some of their good friends [from Leyden] into this purchase if they pleased, and to deal with them for moneys at better rates, etc.

Touching which I shall here insert a letter of Mr. Sherley's giving light to what followed thereof:

> ... It is true that your engagements are great, not only the purchase, but you are yet necessitated to take up the stock you work upon, and that not at 6 or 8% as it is here let out, but at 30, 40, yea and some at 50%. Which, were not your gains great, and God's blessing on your honest endeavor more than ordinary, it could not be that you should long subsist in the maintaining of and upholding of your worldly affairs. And this your honest and discreet agent Mr. Allerton hath seriously considered, and deeply laid to our minds how to ease you of it. He told me you were contented to accept of me, and some few others to join with you in the purchase as partners, for which I kindly thank you and all the rest, and do willingly accept it.

> ... (We are now agreed) You are eased of the high rate you were at the other two years. I say we leave it freely to yourselves to allow us what you please as God shall bless.

I also, see by your letter, you desire I should be your agent or factor here. I have ever found you so faithful, honest, and upright men as I have even resolved with myself - God assisting me - to do you all the good that lieth in my power.

... Your charge shall be no more, for it is not your salary makes me undertake your business. Thus, commending you and yours, and all God's people, unto the guidance and protection of the Almighty.

London, November 17, 1628

With this letter they sent a draught of a formal deputation to be here sealed, and sent back unto them to authorize them as their agents.

... Mr. Allerton having settled all things, thus, in a good and hopeful way, he made haste to return in the first of the Spring, to be here with their supply for trade for the fishermen.

... He brought a reasonable supply of goods for the Plantation: shoes, leather, cloth and Irish stockings, pitch, tar, ropes and twine; knives, scissors and rowel; rugs, coarse, thick, woolen cloth; lead, shot and powder; hatchets, hoes, axes, scythes, reaphooks, shovels, spades, saws, files, nails and iron pots, drugs and spices; total L232 and without those great interest as before is noted; and **brought an account of the beaver sold and how the money was disposed for goods, and the payment of other debts; having paid all debts abroad to others,** save to Mr. Sherley, Mr. Beauchamp and Mr. Andrews. **So now they had no more foreign debts but the abovesaid.**

... Also he brought them further notice that their friends ... and some others that would join with them in the trade and purchase, **did intend for to send over to Leyden for a competent number of them to be here next year** without fail, if the Lord pleased to bless their journey.

He also brought them a patent for fishing at Kennebec but it was so strait, and ill bounded as they were fain to renew and enlarge it next year.

Hitherto, Mr. Allerton did them good and faithful service, and well had it been, if he had so continued, or else they had not now ceased to employing him any longer, thus, into England. But of this more afterwards.

Having procured a patent (as is above said) for Kennebec,

they now erected a house up above in the river in the most convenient place for trade, and furnished the same with commodities for that end, both winter and summer.

... This year the Dutch sent again unto them from their Plantation both kind letters, and also divers commodities, as sugar, linen cloth, Holland [cheese], finer and coarser stuffs. They came up with their bark to Manomet, to their house there, in which came their secretary DeRasieres, who was accompanied with a noise of trumpeters, and some other attendants, and desired that they would send a boat for him, for he could not travel so far overland. So they sent a boat to Scusset and brought him to the Plantation with the chief of his company. And after some few days entertainment, he returned to his bark, and some of them went with him and brought sundry of his goods. After which beginning, thus made, they sent oftentimes to the same place and had intercourse together for divers years. [In a letter to the Dutch West Indies Company DeRasieres noted that the Pilgrims give the Indian tribes an example of better ordinances and a better life than the Dutch of Manhattan.]

... But that which turned most to their profit was an entrance into the trade of wampumpeag. For they now bought about L50 worth of it of them, and they told them how vendible it was at their Fort Orania [Fort Orange-later Albany], and did persuade them, they would find it so at Kennebec ... And strange it was to see the great alteration it made in a few years among the Indians themselves; for all the Indians, of these parts and the Massachusetts, had none or very little of it, but the Sachems and some special persons that wore a little of it for ornament ... the Narragansetts do gather the shells of which they make it from their shores. And it hath now continued a current commodity these twenty years.

... This year Mr. Allerton brought over a young man for a minister to the people here, whether upon his own head or at the motion of friends there I well know not. But it was without the Church's sending, for they had been so bitten by Mr. Lyford as they desired to know the person well, whom they should invite amongst them. His name was Mr. Rogers, but they perceived upon some trial that he was crazed in his brain, so they were fain to be at further charge to send him back again the next year, and lose all the charge that was expended in his hither bringing.

... Mr Allerton in the years before had brought over some small quantity of goods upon his own particular, and sold them for his own private benefit, which was more than any man had yet hitherto attempted. But because he had otherwise done them good service and also, because he sold them among the people at the Plantation, by which their wants were supplied, and alleging it was the love of Mr. Sherley and some other friends that would needs trust him with some goods, and conceiving it might do him some good and none hurt; so it was not much looked at but passed over.

But this year he brought over a greater quantity, and they were so intermixed with the goods from the General, as they knew not which were theirs and which was his, being packed up together ... Yet, because love thinks no evil nor is suspicious, they took his fair words for excuse, and resolved to send him again this year for England, considering how well, he had done the former business, and what good acceptation he had with their friends there; as also, seeing sundry of their friends from Leyden were sent for, which would or might be much furthered by his means.

... And [as he left for England] in his instructions they bound him to bring over no goods on their account, but L50 in hose and shoes, and some linen cloth, as they were bound by covenant, when they took the trade; also some trading goods to such a value, **and in no case to exceed his instructions nor run them into any further charge,** he well knowing how their state stood. Also, that he should so provide that their trading goods come over betimes; and whatsoever was sent on their account should be packed up by itself, marked with their mark, and no other goods to be mixed with theirs. Forso, he prayed them to give him such instructions, as they saw good, and he would follow them to prevent any jealousy, or further offense, upon the former forementioned dislikes.

XX *Arrivals from Leyden and Heavy Expenses*

William Bradford - Anno Domini 1629

Mr. Allerton safely arriving in England and delivering his letters to their friends there and acquainting them with his instructions, found good acception with them, and they were ... willing to join with them in the partnership of trade, and in the charge to send over the Leyden people; a company whereof were already come out of Holland, and [were] prepared to come over, so were sent away before Mr. Allerton could be ready to come. They had passage with the ships that came to Salem that brought over many goodly persons to begin the Plantation and Churches of Christ there [five or six ships brought about 350 settlers to Salem that spring and summer, and also to the Bay of Massachusetts].

So their long stay, and keeping back was recompensed by the Lord to their friends here with a double blessing; in that they not only enjoyed them now beyond their late expectation – when all their hopes seem to be cut off – but [there] were with them many more godly friends and Christian brethren, as the beginning of a larger harvest unto the Lord.

In the increase of His churches and people in these parts, to the admiration of many, and almost wonder of the world, that **of so small beginnings so great things should ensue**, as time after manifested. And that here should be a resting place for so many of the Lord's people, when so sharp a scourge came upon their own nation [England]. But it was the Lord's doing, and it ought to be marvellous in our eyes.

... That I may handle things, together, I have put these two companies that came from Leyden in this place. Though they came at two several times, yet they both came out of England this year. The former company, being 35 persons were shipped in May, and arrived here about August. The latter were shipped in the beginning of March and arrived here the latter end of May 1630, (in the *Lyon*, William Peirce, master, coming from Bristol to Salem). Mr. Sherley's two letters, the effect whereof I have before related, as much of them as is pertinent, mentions both.

Their charge, as Mr. Allerton brought it in afterwards on account, came to above L500, besides their fetching hither from Salem and the Bay, where they and their goods were landed; viz., their transportation from Holland to England and their charges lying there and passage hither with clothing provided for them. For I find by account **for the one company**, 125 yards of jersey, 127 ellons (45 inches) of linen cloth, shoes 66 pair, with many other particulars. The charge of the other company is reckoned on the several families; some L50, some L40, and some L30, and so more or less, as their number and expenses were.

And besides all this charge, their friends and Brethren here were to provide corn and other provisions for them till they could reap a crop. Those that came in May were thus maintained upward of 16 or 18 months before they had any harvest of their own, and the other by proportion. And all they could do in the meantime was to get them some housing and prepare them grounds to plant on, against the season ... These things I note, for sundry regards.

First, to show **a rare example, herein of brotherly love and Christian care, in performing their promises and covenants to their brethren,** to, and in a sort beyond their power; that they should venture so desperately to engage themselves to accomplish this thing, and bear it so cheerfully. **For they never demanded, much less had any repayment of all these great sums, thus disbursed.**

Secondly, it must needs be that there was more than of man in these achievement that should thus readily stir up the hearts of such able friends to join in partnership with them, in such a case, and cleave so faithfully to them, as these did in so great adventures. And the more because the most of them never saw their faces to this day, there being neither kindred, alliance, or other acquaintance or relations between any of them than hath been before mentioned. It must needs be therefore the special work and hand of God.

Thirdly, **that these poor people here in a wilderness should not withstanding be enabled in time to repay all these engagements,** and many more unjustly brought upon them through the unfaithfulness of some, and many other great losses, which they sustained. Which will be made manifest, if the Lord be pleased to give life and time.

... The Leyden people being thus come over, and sundry of the Generality, seeing and hearing how great the charge was like to be ... they began to murmer and repine at it.

... Especially, at the paying of the three bushels of corn a year, according to the former agreement, when the trade was let for six years as was aforesaid. But to give them content, herein, also it was promised them, that if they could do it in the time without it, they would never demand it of them, which gave them good content. And indeed, it never was paid, as will appear by the sequel.

... Concerning the rest of Mr. Allerton's instructions in which they strictly enjoined him not to exceed above that L50 in the goods before mentioned; not to bring any but trading commodities, he followed them not at all but did quite the contrary, bringing over many other sorts of retail goods, selling what he could by the way on his own account, and delivering the rest, which he said to be theirs into the store. And for trading goods, brought but little in comparison; excusing the matter - they had laid out much about the Leyden people and Patent, etc; and for other goods they had much of them of their own dealings, without present disbursement ... And for passing his bounds and instructions, he laid it on Mr. Sherley.

... By this it appears that there was a kind of concurrence between Mr. Allerton and them [the Adventurers] in these things and they gave more regard to his way and course in these things, than to the advice from hence, which made him bold to presume above his instructions, and to run on in the course he did, to their greater hurt afterwards ... Another more secret cause was herewith concurrent. Mr. Allerton had married the daughter of their Reverend Elder, Mr. Brewster, a man beloved and honoured amongst them, and who took great pains in teaching and dispensing the Word of

God unto them—whom they were loath ... to any way offend, so as they bore with much in that respect.

... That neither he nor any other did intend to charge the general account with anything that ran in particular, or that Mr. Sherley or any other did purpose, but that the general should be first and fully supplied. I say charity makes me thus conceive, though things fell out otherwise, and they missed of their aims, and the general suffered abundantly hereby, as will afterwards appear.

... I had like to have omitted another passage that fell out the beginning of this year. There was one Mr. Ralph Smith and his wife and family that came over into the Bay of Massachusetts, and sojourned at present with some straggling people that lived at Nantasket. Here being a boat of this place, putting in there on some occasion, he earnestly desired that they would give him his passage for Plymouth, and some such things as they could well carry; having heard he might procure house room ... Should he resolve to settle there, or else where as God should dispose, for he was weary of being in the uncouth place and in a poor house that would neither keep him nor his goods dry.

So, seeing him to be a grave man and understood he had been a minister, though they had no order for such a thing, yet they presumed and brought him. He was accordingly kindly entertained and housed, and the rest of his goods and servants sent for. He exercised his gifts amongst them, and afterwards was chosen into the ministry, and so remained for sundry years. [Ralph Smith was a scholar of Christ's College, Cambridge and a Separatist. He was ordained the first pastor of the Plymouth Chruch, before the end of 1629.]

It was before noted that sundry of these that came from Leyden came over in the ships that came to Salem where Mr. John Endecott had chief command. (Mr. Endecott, a worthy gentleman brought over a patent under the broad seal for the government of the Massachusetts).

An infection that grew among the passengers at sea, spread also among them ashore, of which many died, some of the scurvy, others of an infectious fever which continued some time amongst them. Our people through God's goodness escaped it.

Governor Endecott wrote hither for some help, understanding

there here was one that had some skill in curing divers of the scurvy and other diseases by letting blood and other means. [This was Samuel Fuller.] The Governor sent him unto them, and wrote a letter, from whom he received an answer. It shows the beginning of their acquaintance, and closing in the truth and ways of God, and their fellowship and church estate there. [Salem was the second church in these parts.]

Being as followeth:

Right Worthy Sir:

... I acknowledge myself much bound to you for your kind love and care in sending Mr. Fuller among us.

And word from another Salem settler, Charles Gott who came out with John Endecott:

... The 20th of July it pleased the Lord to move the heart of our Governor to set apart a solemn day of humiliation for the choice of a pastor and teacher ... They acknowledged there was a twofold calling, **the one an inward calling**, *when the Lord moved the heart of man; ...* **the second was an outward calling** *which was from the people, when a company of believers are joined together in covenant to walk in all the ways of God.*

... I hope that you will say ... that here was a right foundation laid.

XXI   Allerton's new Venture; the Massachusetts Bay Colony Takes Form

William Bradford - Anno Domini 1630

... They looked earnestly for a timely supply this Spring, by the fishing ship which they expected, and had been at charge to keep a stage for her; but none came nor was any supply heard of for them.

... At last they heard of Mr. Peirce's arrival in the Bay of the Massachusetts, who brought passengers and goods thither. They presently sent a shallop, conceiving they should have something by him ... But he told them he had none. [This was on the *White Angel*] [Also] they learned that a ship was set out on fishing, but after 11 week's beating at sea, she met with such foul weather as she was faced back again for England, and the season being over gave up the voyage. Neither did he hear of much goods in her for the Plantation, or that she did belong to them; for he had heard something from Mr. Allerton tending that way. But Mr. Allerton had bought another ship, and was to come in her and was to fish for bass to the eastward, and to bring goods, etc. These things did much trouble them, and half astonish them. Mr. Winslow having been to the eastward brought news of the like things with some more particulars, and that it was likely Mr. Allerton would be late, before he came.

At length, they having an opportunity, resolved to send Mr. Winslow with what beaver they had ready into England to see how the squares went, being very jealous of these things and Mr. Allerton's courses. And [they] writ such letters and gave him such instructions as they thought meet; and **if he found things not well to**

discharge Mr. Allerton for being any longer agent for them, or to deal any more in the business, and to see how the accounts stood.

About the middle of summer arrives Mr. Timothy Hatherley in the Bay of Massachusetts, being one of the partners, who had come over in the same ship that was set out on fishing [called the *Friendship*]. They presently sent to him, making no question but now they had goods come, and should know how all things stood. But they found the former news true, how this ship had been so long at sea, and spent and spoiled her provisions and overthrown the voyage. And he, being sent over by the rest of the partners to see how things went there, being at Bristol with Mr. Allerton, in the ship bought [*White Angel*] and ready to set sail; overnight came a messenger from Barnstaple to Mr. Allerton, and told him of the return of the Ship and what had befallen. And he not knowing what to do, having a great charge under hand, the Ship lying at his rates and now ready to set sail, got him to go and discharge the Ship (of her fisherman crew) and take order for the goods.

To be short, they found Mr. Hatherley something reserved, and troubled in himself (Mr. Allerton not being there) not knowing how to dispose of the goods till he came. But he heard the news of the arrival of the other ship to the eastward (*White Angel*) and expected his coming. But he told them there was not much for them in this ship, only two packs of Barnstaple rugs, and two hogsheads of metheglin (herbs boiled in honey and fermented), drawn out in wooden flackets (small kegs). But when these flackets came to be received, there was left but six gallons of the two hogsheads, it being drunk up under the name leakage and so lost. But the ship was filled with goods for sundry gentlemen and others that were come to plant in the Massachusetts, for which they paid freight by the ton. And this was all the satisfaction they could have at present. So they brought this small parcel of goods and returned with this news and a letter so obscure, which made them much marvel thereat.

The letter was as followeth:

> *Gentlemen, Partners and Loving Friends:*
> *We have this year set forth a fishing ship and a trading ship, which latter we have bought; and so have disbursed a great deal of money as will appear by the accounts. And because this ship is to act two parts;*

fishing for bass and trading; and that while Mr. Allerton was employed about the trading, the fishing might suffer by carelessness, we have entreated your and our loving friend Mr. Hatherley to go over with him, knowing he will be a comfort to Mr. Allerton, a joy to you to see a careful and loving friend, and a great stay to the business. And so a great content to us. That if it should please God, the one should fail, as God forbid, yet the other would keep both reckonings and things upright. For we are now out great sums of money, as they will acquaint you withal, etc. When we were out but four or five hundred points apiece, we looked not much after it but left it to you and your agent ... But now we are out double, nay treble apiece, some of us. Which makes us both write and send over our friend Mr. Hatherley, whom we pray you to enteratain kindly of which we doubt not of.

The main end of sending him is to see the state and account of all the business, of all which we pray you inform him fully, though the ship and business wait for it and him. For we should take it very unkindly that we should entreat him to take such a journey, and that when it pleaseth God he returns, he could not give us content, and satisfaction in this particular, through default of any of you. But we hope you will so order your business, as neither he nor we shall have cause to complain, but to do, as we have ever done, think well of you all.

Yours,

James Sherley
March 25, 1631

It needs not be thought strange that these things should amaze and trouble them; first, that this fishing ship should be set out, and fraught with other men's goods, and scarce any of theirs, seeing their main end was - as is before remembered - to bring them a full supply, and their special order not to set out any, except this was done. And now a ship to come on their account, clean contrary, to their both end and order, was a mystery they could not understand. And so much the worse, seeing she had such ill success as to lose both her voyage and provisions. The second thing, that another ship should be bought and sent out on new designs, a thing not so much as once thought on by any either by word or letter ... As **for Mr. Allerton to follow any trade for them, it was never in their thoughts**. And thirdly, that their friends should complain of disbursements, and yet run into such great things, and charge of shipping and new projects of their own heads, not only without but against all order and advice, was to them very strange. And fourthly, that all these matters of so great charge and employments should be thus wrapped up in a brief and obscure letter; they knew not what to make of it.

But amidst all their doubts they must have patience till Mr. Allerton and Mr. Hatherley should come. In the meantime, Mr. Winslow was gone for England; and others of them were forced to follow their employments with the best means they had, till they could hear of better.

At length, Mr. Hatherley and Mr. Allerton came unto them - after they had delivered goods - and found them stricken with some sadness about these things; Mr. Allerton told them that the ship White Angel did not belong to them nor their account, neither need they have anything to do with her except they would. And Mr. Hatherley confirmed the same, and said that they would have had him to have had a part, but he refused.

... Mr. Hatherley fully understanding the state of all things, had good satisfaction, and could well inform them how all things stood between Mr. Allerton and the Plantation. Yea, he found that Mr. Allerton had got within him, and got all the goods into his own hands, for which Mr. Hatherley stood jointly engaged to them here, about the ship Friendship as also most of the freight money, besides some of his own particular estate, about which more will appear hereafter. So he returned to England, and they sent a good quantity of beaver with him to the rest of the partners; so both he and it were very welcome unto them.

... **Mr. Allerton followed his affairs and returned with his White Angel, being no more employed by the Plantation**. But these businesses were not ended till many years after, now well understood of a long time, but folded up in obscurity and kept in the clouds, to the great loss and vexation of the Plantation, who in the end were - for peace sake - forced to bear the unjust burden of them almost to their undoing. [It was 1645 before this long and tedious business was concluded between the partners here and them in England.]

They sent letters also by Mr. Hatherley to the partners there to show them how Mr. Hatherley and Mr. Allerton had discharged them of the Friendship's account, and that they both affirmed that the White Angel did not at all belong to them, and therefore, desired that their account might not be charged therewith. Also, they writ to Mr. Winslow, their agent, that he in like manner should in their names protest against it, if any such thing should be intended; for they would never yield to the same. As, also, to signify to them that **they renounced Mr. Allerton wholly for being their agent, or to have anything to do in any of their business.**

[Meanwhile, as noted, the Massachusetts Bay Colony was beginning to take form. John Endecott, bearing a patent for "The Massachusetts", landed in 1628 at Salem to establish a settlement. He served as governor until the following year when Governor John Winthrop arrived with a fleet of five vessels at Charlestown (later Boston) and sufficient passengers to swell the settlement to over 350 persons.

These were Puritans who, by now, were fleeing church oppression in England. They sought to emulate their Pilgrim brethren, whom they had earlier castigated for leaving the Church of England and the mother country.

As reported in the Bradford text, the Endecott and Winthrop vessels also brought over substantial reinforcements from the Leyden congregation for the Plymouth colony. Nevertheless, the Pilgrims now had the competition and stimulating effect of a much larger and wealthier nearby plantation.

Winthrop also brought with him his own ideas for governing, and these were not those of the Pilgrims. This important distinction was set forth in *March of Freedom* by William Harlan Hale:

He told his flock, 'If you will be satisfied to enjoy such civil and lawful liberties, such as Christ allows you, then you will quietly and cheerfully submit unto authority which is set over you. ... for your own good.'

But this was the very opposite of what had been expressed in the Mayflower Compact, drawn up in the Mayflower's cabin some years before. Their state was based not on orders from above but on the pledge of everyman.

The Puritan leaders who only recently had been in opposition against the church tyranny had now established an even more complete church tyranny. You could not vote unless you were a member of their official church.

At the conclusion of Chapters XX and XXI, Bradford

included a number of letters detailing relations of the two colonies. Thus, Governor Endecott revealed in a letter to the Plymouth governor that he had heard rumors that the Pilgrims were rigid separatists and that he was glad to find that they were not.

Other correspondence indicated that the Puritans were uncertain whether they would be received by coolness, even hostility, by the Pilgrims. Bradford responded with friendship and sent the physician, Samuel Fuller, to Salem to aid and advise the embryo colony during a period of initial serious illness among arriving passengers, apparently traceable to the confined shipboard quarters and the long voyage from England. The Pilgrims had experienced a "great illness" of the same or greater intensity after disembarking from the Mayflower.

Endecott expressed the hope that they could maintain relations with the Church of England, a desire later abandoned by the Bay Colony which embraced the Congregationalist example of Plymouth.

The importance of cultivating good relations had been emphasized to both the Salem and the Charlestown contingents by John Cotton, celebrated Puritan minister, who charged them to take the advice of those at Plymouth and do nothing to offend them. Taking note of sentiment in the Bay Colony, Dr. Fuller wrote in August, 1630:

Here are divers honest Christians that are desirous to see us, some out of love which they bear to us, and the good persuasion they have of us; others to see whether we be so ill as they had heard of us.

We have a name of holiness, and love of God, and His saints. The Lord make us more answerable, and that it be more than a name, or else it will do us no good.

Edward Winslow and Dr. Fuller reported that Governor Winthrop had written from Charlestown: *manifesting the hand of God to be upon them at Plymouth and against them at Charlestown, in visiting them with sickness and taking divers from amongst them, not sparing the righteous but partaking with the wicked in those bodily judgements.*

It was concluded that the Lord was to be sought in righteousness; and to that end a day set apart that they might humble themselves before God and seek him in His ordinances. That such Godly persons who are amongst them and known to each other should publicly make known their Godly desire and practice the same, viz: solemnly to enter into covenant with the Lord to walk in His Ways.

And since they lived in three distant places, each having men of ability amongst them ... they earnestly entreated that the Church of Plymouth set apart the same day to the same ends, beseeching the Lord to withdraw his hand of correction from them [at Charlestown and Salem] so as also to establish and direct them in His ways.

Thus the Plymouth plantation was recognized, not only as a going and successful colony, but as a friend, adviser and brother to the new and already much larger Bay Colony. Bradford took note and exulted with pride in this eloquent passage]:

Thus, out of small beginnings, greater things have been produced by His hand that made all things of nothing, and gives being to all things that are; as one small candle may light a thousand, so the Light here kindled hath shone unto many, yea, in some sort to our Whole Nation; let the glorious name of Jehovah have all the praise.

Part Four

A People Capable of Greatness

Some Assessments and Re–evaluation of the Record

Commentaries "A" through "G"
By Adelia White Notson and Robert Carver Notson

"A people capable of greatness will not forget the virtues of their forefathers. Reverently will they cherish them and gratefully present them in all their luster for the respect and imitation of after ages."
Col. John T. Heard at the laying of the cornerstone, National
Monument to the Forefathers at Plymouth, August 2, 1859.

Commentary "A"

How and Why the Pilgrims were Kept in Financial Bondage

The basic story has now been told by the Pilgrims in their own words. The colony has been brought through its period of debt and dependency.

The concluding chapters of our presentation have told the incredible and confusing story of how the colony finally undertook to discharge itself of its obligations to its sponsors, and free itself of the ineptitude and chicanery of its London agents. The original contract was for seven years but matters dragged on for 25 years. It must have appeared that the settlers never would be free of obligations.

In addition, it seems quite clear that they paid off their debt many times over but were held in financial subjection:

1. By the juggling of their accounts and enforcement of terms to which they had not agreed and to which they frequently objected.

2. By the refusal or failure of their agents and sponsors to follow instructions.

3. By the charging of their accounts with costs and losses over which they had no control and frequently generated by transactions they had not authorized.

4. Finally, by the refusal of James Sherley, their last agent and one of the Adventurers, to give an accounting either to the colony or to his associates.

Matters were brought to a head by what in this day would be regarded as conflict of interest, embezzlement, and fraud.

The colony got together a large shipment of pelts, representing 3,678 pounds of beaver and 466 skins of otter, mink, and black foxes.

It represented a fortune in furs, and Governor Bradford calculated that it would not only pay off the debt but leave them a return of some L2200. But, they could get no accounting of it from Sherley. Further, his two associates, Richard Andrews and John Beauchamp, could obtain no settlement and said they had had no money for two years. They appealed to the colony to protect their interests. With the usual soft-heartedness, the colonists sent them L434 and 1325 pounds of beaver. Beauchamp disposed of his half at a profit of L400. Andrews handled his half ineptly and lost L40.

To whom was the loss charged? To the Pilgrims, as usual. But the colonists had no "other cheek" to turn. They dismissed Sherley and demanded a final settlement. Matters dragged on for some years with Sherley calling for more furs and the other two claiming balances due. The Adventurers, through Massachusetts Bay, did manage to milk another L544 and some property out of the colony.

At that point, 1645, relations were concluded, the cruel financial charade ended. The colony took up a trade with the Dutch in Manhattan, and with others.

Undoubtedly, the problems of the Plymouth colonists were compounded by their extreme necessities, which left most of the bargaining power in the hands of their principals in London. There was the lack of communications. There was the anxiety to bring over relatives and friends from Leyden.

The Adventurers took advantage of them in two other ways: They imposed a charge of 30% on moneys advanced to bring over members of the Leyden group. Then, instead of following instructions, they sent over many persons not suited to and not desired by the colony—all at the latter's expense.

The inexperience of Bradford – otherwise a very able man – in business, and his Christian charity and faith in the good intentions of others played its part. John Carver had been a merchant and had acquired considerable substance. He was not about to let the Adventurers get away with pushing him around. If he had lived, events might have taken an easier course.

We have presented the main story, but the student may pursue further details in concluding chapters of Bradford's *Of Plymouth Plantation* and other writings. This much is sufficient to our purpose.

Commentary "B"

Myths of the Pilgrim Story

Certain legends and errors have grown up around the Pilgrim story. Before concluding, we desire to deal with some of these ideas. Many of them have been the outgrowth of fictionalized versions. Others have emerged from careless or inadequate reading.

We also desire to place evaluation on some facts of the story, and some backgrounds, as we have observed them.

It is important that we first examine some of the myths which persist in the public mind:

The myth: The Pilgrims constituted the first band of Puritans to settle in Massachusetts.

This is probably the most persistent myth extant regarding the Mayflower Colonists which settled in New Plymouth. The Pilgrims were not Puritans. A brief background is needed to make the statement clear — a point on which there has been general confusion.

The early church of the Christians in the countries of western Europe was Roman Catholic. It became powerful, propertied, and corrupt. The reformation had been sweeping continental Europe and was expressed in formation of various Protestant churches. Among the English, John Wycliffe had raised his voice to demand reform but his strictures were suppressed for a century and a half.

The reformation in England came afoul of Henry VIII's marital vagaries and consequent clashes with the church. The king chose to cut the ties with Rome (1536) and set up the Church of England with himself at its head. He did permit the placement of the Bible in the churches, where it was read and interpreted by the laity, as well as the clergy. But he maintained the authority of the bishops and the rituals of the church.

Soon three factions developed:

1. The Conformists, or high ritualists.
2. The Non-Conformists, or broad church "puritans".
3. The Separatists, popularly called Brownists after Robert Brown, the Separatist crusader.

The Conformists insisted on maintaining the authority and rituals of the church unchanged. The Non-Conformists, who became known derisively as "Puritans", believed in reforming or purifying the church from within. They believed in democracy in the church and in politics. The Separatists gave up on the church and decided to go their own way, and worship God according to their own consciences. The Puritans and the Separatists shared many doctrinal views, including simplification of church forms and government, but they differed on discipline.

By the time the Scrooby church had evolved, private judgment was almost everywhere denied and toleration of religious differences was denounced. The crown enacted decrees to punish those who did not conform. Failure to attend approved Church of England services could bring fines, imprisonment, and death.

Singularly enough, many of the Puritan clergy joined in denouncing the Separatists. A majority of the lower clergy and middle-classes appeared to favor Puritanism and they advocated putting the church into the hands of the people.

Because the church and state were not distinguishable in many ways, these Puritans also favored political democratic expression. They supplied leaders in movements to increase the authority of Parliament at the expense of the throne. The Separatists agreed on these objectives but held little influence in the matter.

By beginning of the 17th century the Separatists were being hounded and harassed unmercifully and began fleeing the country or going underground. The Scrooby colony, by then known to themselves as Pilgrims, went to Holland and then many of them to America.

Wrote Frank M. Gregg in his *Founding of a Nation*:

That the Pilgrims and Puritans were not one and the same has been recognized by students of American history but the average person still thinks of them as one people. There are many points of similarity: They were men of the Bible and men of exact consciences.

It is essential to discriminate between them. The Pilgrims came to America to enjoy religious freedom. The Puritans came to America to enjoy political as well as religious freedom.

The Pilgrims were simple country folk. They were not acquainted with trades nor traffic but had been used to a plain country life and the innocent trade of husbandry.

The Puritans included many of the gentry and personages of wealth and influence.

The Pilgrims were modest; the Puritans more aristocratic.

Eventually, the Puritans were to withdraw from the Church of England and the Pilgrims were to be absorbed into the Massachusetts Bay Colony, which had been the Puritan stronghold.

The Myth: The Pilgrims were communists.

This canard keeps appearing from time to time with very little to sustain it. In fact, a careful reading of the literature turns up evidence directly to the contrary. Circumstances and their sponsors did dictate that the colonists should start out with a communal arrangement. They paid in their money to purchase common stock in the enterprise, referred to as the "General".

This was necessary in order to hire the *Mayflower* and to purchase provisions for the trip and afterwards.

It was also necessary to bind the entire group to repayment of the advances from the "Adventurers" by encumbering all property and the labors of all the colonists for at least seven years.

When they arrived in the New World their supplies had to be hoarded and most carefully dispensed in order that they might eke out an existence. Otherwise, improvidence by some would have placed all in jeopardy.

But representations that the Pilgrims subscribed to the communistic doctrine of common property are in error. In the first place, they never practiced it in Leyden. In the second place, they strenuously resisted dictates of the Adventurers that all work and all property, even their lands and homes, should go into the common holdings until the debts were paid.

Pastor Robinson and John Carver forecast that the colonists

would work better and produce more if some of their time (two days a week) could be "on their own account" and on improving their homes, if the houses belonged to them individually.

The experience of the Pilgrims in this regard is one of the classic lessons of history, showing how the doctrine of common property breaks down under test. No communistic society has long existed without compulsion because it runs counter to human desire.

Even in this situation, where the strongest of religious altruism and motivation existed and where the threat of famine spurred them to their tasks, still the system proved inadequate.

And so, in Chapter XIV Bradford recited how the shift from a communal to a private enterprise regime brought beneficial results. At that point, 1623, they decided that they could make a partial change, in the expectation that the yield of corn would be increased. And so it proved, after each man was allowed to plant for himself.

"This," reported Bradford, "had very good success for it made all hands very industrious, so as much more corn was planted than otherwise would have been by any other means ... and saved a great deal of trouble and gave far better content."

As long as the corn went into the common storehouse, many of the women complained of weakness. But now they went willingly to the fields, where before to have ordered them to work would have been "thought great tyranny and oppression."

No motivation as great has ever been found to get men to work and produce as that they may individually improve their lot. Bradford pointed to these results to prove that even among "godly and sober men" the system evinced the "vanity of that conceit of Plato's ... that the taking away of property, and bringing into community ... would make them happy and flourishing—as if they were wiser than God ... But they deemed it a kind of slavery ... God, in his wisdom, saw another course better for them."

So much for the false idea that the Pilgrims embraced communism: they resisted it.

Some 360 years later Communist China was to learn much the same lesson. By easing the commune system and permitting farmers to profit personally by tilling extra acreages, the Central Committee found that it could greatly increase agricultural production.

Meanwhile, Soviet Communists in the 1980s remained bogged in a collectivist system that has failed miserably to feed their people. As a result, Russia has been buying millions of tons of grain from the United States and other countries.

The Pilgrims steered the embryo American nation down the successful road of individual enterprise and ownership.

The myth: The Pilgrims engaged in witch hunts.

Belief in witchcraft was widespread in Europe and other parts of the world in the 16th, 17th and 18th centuries. It was stimulated by Pope Innocent VIII. One of his agents claimed that he had burned 900 witches. In the 16th century, it has been estimated, some 100,000 lives were taken on allegations of witchcraft.

England accounted for many of these. James I wrote a book urging the church to deal severely with witches. Several American colonies became infected, especially Massachusetts Bay Colony. In Salem, where the hysteria centered in 1692, some 55 pleaded guilty and were spared, on the theory that their confessions tended to purge them of guilt. Nineteen pleaded not guilty and were hanged.

New Plymouth did not wholly escape the contagion. On her books was a law decreeing death for witches.

In 1661 a case arose. Dinah, wife of Joseph Sylvester, denounced her neighbor as a witch. She said she saw the wife of William Holmes conversing with the devil, in the form of a bear. Governor Thomas Prence presided over the General Court. She told an apparently sensational and preposterous story.

The court not only acquitted Mrs. Holmes but found Mrs. Sylvester guilty of slander. She was publicly whipped. That put an end to such accusations for 16 years.

In 1677 an elderly woman, Mrs. Thomas (Mary) Ingham was accused of being a witch. It was alleged that she had conspired with the devil to cause a young girl to have fits. A jury found no guilt.

While the delusion persisted elsewhere, New Plymouth had no witch, no hanging.

The myth: The Pilgrims were rigid, harsh, intolerant and bigoted.

Were the Pilgrims a bigoted and intolerant band? In all fairness, they must be measured against the harshness of the society from which they came, not against the permissiveness of three and a half centuries later.

They were men of high, fixed religious and moral principles. And they were exacting of themselves in the practice of these beliefs. They fled first to Holland and then to America in order to worship God according to their consciences. Did they deny similar rights to others?

There is good evidence that they were willing to accord liberty of thought and conscience to others—a most remarkable virtue for their day. Goodwin in his *Pilgrim Republic* had this to say:

The Pilgrims were not repressive ... The Pilgrim Fathers heartily welcomed to their little state all men of other sects, who adhered to the essentials of Christianity and who were ready to conform to the local laws and customs.

They were in advance of their brethren in England; much in advance of ... their sister colony of Massachusetts ... they were more tolerant.

At the Lord's table they communed with pious Episcopalians, with Calvinists of the French and Dutch churches and with Presbyterians, and recognized the spiritual fraternity of all who held the (Christian) faith.

The contrast is well illustrated in the somewhat surprising story of Myles Standish. Captain Standish was a career soldier from Lancashire, England, and Isle of Man employed by the Holland military during the war with Spain.

He visited with Robinson and Brewster, became impressed with the Pilgrim colony, and at 36 years of age joined the expedition to the New World. He was small of stature, red-headed, and hot-tempered. He was sixth signer of the Mayflower Compact. The security of the plantation was placed in his hands and he discharged his duty with distinction.

He was a stalwart citizen of the Plymouth settlement, a member of the governing board, a land commissioner and founder of Duxbury.

Goodwin in *Pilgrim Republic* states that Myles Standish came from a well-placed Roman Catholic family, a member of which had been a bishop at the time of Henry VIII. Suggestion that Standish had been a practicing Catholic was called into question by one modern researcher. But, it appears that Standish never joined the

Plymouth church. Even more significantly, although he attended services and adhered to the principles of the church, he declined to accept communion.

It is known that Standish counseled toleration in religious matters. It is also evident from his high place on the General Court that the colony not only accepted his religious divergence but shared his toleration.

For themselves, the Pilgrims held to a strong faith but little formal creed.

At this time Massachusetts Bay Colony restricted the franchise to members of the church. It also made attendance on public worship compulsory. Church attendance at Plymouth was voluntary, but expected. Right to vote did not depend on church membership.

Authorities agree that New Plymouth welcomed all law-abiding men in search of a home, at least some of whom had been expelled from Massachusetts Bay Colony—and somewhat to the annoyance of the latter.

Some 35 or 40 years later this spirit of tolerance was severely tested by bands of provocative evangelizers who forced their way into the colonies. They undertook disruption of churches, defying all control and breaking up services with violent demonstrations. Seemingly strange from this point of time, they were early converts of George Fox, Quaker evangelist.

In the Massachusetts Bay Colony confrontations were frequent, with vociferous abuse and clamor being heaped on preachers and congregations.

Massachusetts Bay undertook harsh measures, including flogging and banishment. Finally, a threat of death was added, but the zealots returned. They were arrested and sentenced to be executed. Authorities pleaded with them to leave, right up to the gallows. They refused, and four were hanged. It appeared they sought martyrdom.

Plymouth took a gentler course. Henry Fell, a Quaker, wrote in 1657 to Margaret Fell in Barbados: "In Plymouth there is a people not so rigid as the others in Boston, and there are great desires among them after the truth."

The fanatics were treated in Plymouth with initial tolerance. Isaac Robinson, son of Reverend John, was appointed on a committee to visit Quaker meetings and reason with them and "endeavor to reduce them from the error of their ways".

Incidents in Plymouth were few. Some disrupters were escorted out of the colony and, when they returned, they were whipped and imprisoned.

Thomas Prence, governor at that time, was inclined to severity but the colony favored moderation. In time, so did the Quakers, who settled at Duxbury, and other points, where they were accepted and protected by their neighbors.

It should be noted that these early zealots were a radical left wing of the movement and that they bore little resemblance to the gentle, pacifistic and non-offensive Quakers, or Friends, of a later day in Pennsylvania and elsewhere.

The Plymouth laws were regarded as mild for their day. And these tended to be further tempered in administration by a rule of reason and a degree of mercy not common to their time.

As we have previously observed, many of the "facts" that most persons "know" about the Pilgrims simply are not true, or are distortions of truth. Part of this arises from the mis-identification of the Pilgrims as Puritans, partly from inadequate ficitionalized and romanticized stories.

Some writers of late have undertaken to ridicule and "debunk" the Plymouth colony. A study of the literature indicates that the Pilgrims were neither as pure as some sentimental stories make them nor as dour and rigid as others assert.

They were human beings of extraordinary quality and achievement but they often reflected some of the weaknesses of the society from which they came. Nevertheless, their heroic mastery of adversity will stand as a benchmark in American annals.

One of the canards hung on the Pilgrims was that they were opposed to sex and repressed it sternly. Hardly an accurate reflection of fact. They had large families. Widowers and widows remarried quickly, sometimes within weeks after the death of a spouse.

They did oppose and punish both illicit sex and perversion. But they believed in normal sex.

Sometimes cartoonists have depicted a blue-nosed, arrogantly prissy person in Puritan costume as the symbol of prohibition and a Puritan woman as a sort of "aunty-everything". There has been a tendency to impute these characteristics to the Pilgrims and the "Pilgrim ethic".

Against this representation, some writers have gleefully placed reports that the Plymouth Colonists brought casks of beer, wine and ale on the *Mayflower*. Actually, these were part of their stores for drinking purposes. They became teetotalers only when these ran out and when they found pure water. Later, they did make their own beer, wine, and also metheglin, fermented honey and water.

But, they believed in sobriety and heavy punishment awaited the over-indulger.

In England under James I some 31 "crimes" were punishable by death, and the number was gradually increased. Before him, under Elizabeth, cruelty had run rampant. Drawing and quartering had been commonplace. At one time over 300 heads were displayed on the entrance to London Bridge.

In fact, the law in England for burning heretics was not repealed until 1677 – 57 years after the Pilgrims landed at Plymouth.

The Massachusetts Bay Colony, settled by the Puritans, prescribed death in 13 offenses, including sacrilege, adultery, false witness, and failure to attend public worship.

By contrast, only five crimes were punishable by death in Plymouth Colony: Treason, murder, diabolical conversation, willful burning of ships or houses, violation and unnatural sex offenses. Enforcement was sparing.

In the early years of the Colony there was record of only one execution—the hanging of John Billington for murder. Up until 1636 the Colony had only 40 laws, mostly enacted for special purposes. Otherwise, the General Court followed the usages of England.

Enforcement of regulations against moral offenses and drunkenness was severe. And punishment for desecration of the Sabbath seems harsh today. Owing to lack of a prison, public whippings and confinement in stocks were used. These were alternatives to fines and were applied with restraint. Repentance frequently brought forgiveness.

The record does not show that the Pilgrims skewered tongues and hanged adulterers, as the Mayflower '70 program stated.

Likewise, the Yankee Traders, who were accused of dealing in African slaves, had the home port of Boston—not Plymouth. Here again is the old confusion of Pilgrims with Puritans. In fact, Captain John Russell, who directed the Plymouth fleet through the early part of the 19th century—to avoid any suspicion of slave trading—ordered that no ship approach the African coast.

The Pilgrims set the pattern of American justice by establishment of the grand jury system and the right of every man to a jury trial.

Writers have stressed that the Pilgrims "stole" the 40 bushels of maize from "Corn Hill" that had been cached there by the Indians. This was, of course, an act of prudent necessity. They behaved like virtually all explorers in a new land, but, unlike the others, they expressed determination to make restitution, and they eventually did so.

Other transgressions have been attributed to Plymouth but let it never be forgotten that more than half of the *Mayflower* manifest was made up of "strangers" recruited by the London company. Subsequent recruits were many of them solid citizens but not a few were adventurers and rascals. Some of the latter were rejected and sent back.

An incident often cited as proof of the dour character of the Pilgrims was the act of Bradford in stopping the play of a group of newly-arrived Anglicans on Christmas day. The reference has been taken out of context.

The Pilgrims had hardly celebrated the bounty of their first harvest in 1621 when the *Fortune* arrived with this new company of settlers entirely without supplies—little but the rags on their backs. Bradford knew from bitter experience that only hard work and sacrifice could see them through the second winter with the added mouths to feed.

Nevertheless, when the Anglicans insisted that they could not work on Christmas because it was a holy day to them, the governor excused them while the rest of the colony went to work. When he found them playing games he "took away their instruments" and sent them home.

It may be true that the Pilgrims did not think that sport was

a proper observance of a holy day but it is likewise true that Bradford faced the necessity of disciplining the group to know that it
was not a company of freeloaders, that others had worked and were
working to keep them alive. Their application and work were required. It was not a whim of Bradford's. It was a grim object lesson,
and a proper one.

**The myth: the Pilgrims seized land from the Indians,
mistreated, and "massacred" the natives.**

The site of the original Plymouth colony was unoccupied and
unclaimed by the natives. As the colony grew, the Pilgrims were
careful to reimburse the Indians for new lands taken over. (As example: a reference in the Carver family lineage reveals that John
Washburn in 1645 "bought land of old Sachem Massasoit for 7 coats,
9 hatchets, 8 hoes, 20 knives, 4 moose skins, 10½ yards of cotton
cloth." This was in Bridgewater where Rebecca Washburn married
Timothy Carver, descendant of Robert Carver, in 1752.)

That the relations of the Pilgrims with the Indians were ex-
emplary was verified by Isaak DeRasieres, secretary of the West In-
dia Company, Manhattan, who wrote after a visit to the colony in
October, 1627:

*The tribes are better conducted than ours, because the English
give them the example of better ordinances and a better life; and who also,
to a certain degree, give them laws by means of the respect they from the
very first have established amongst them.*

Only after later settlers stirred up hostilities did the Pilgrims
take up arms to defend their colony from attack and to aid their
Indian friends. Some authors have been critical of a punitive action
by Captain Myles Standish against leaders of an Indian federation
to the north — the "only blot on the Pilgrims' record" of Indian
relations.

Massasoit, Indian chieftain of a neighboring tribe, had
reported to the plantation that these Indians were plotting to wipe
out a small colony of English rascals at Wessagusset and then attack Plymouth. Massasoit said he had declined to join the plot and
advised preventive steps.

Although the Wessagusset men had been known to mistreat
and threaten the Indians, giving cause for hostility, Standish felt he

could not permit the massacre of an English colony and subsequent attack on his own.

Taking a force of eight armed men, he surprised and executed the Indian leaders and chased the Massachusetts tribe into a swamp. He displayed an Indian skull on the stockade fence of the colony for years.

At least one writer suggests that the attack was really unprovoked and that Edward Winslow, Standish, and Bradford used the story of a plot against the two colonies:

To intimidate the Indians and to drive away the roistering men of Wessagusset who were corrupting the natives, living with their women folk, giving them strong drink, and stealing their food and furs.

To interrupt the improvident trade of the colony with the Indians — in other words, for business reasons.

The action may seem pretty brutal by modern standards, especially against the strong religious backgrounds of the Pilgrims. But, who in this day can say what he might have considered necessary and proper at that time to protect this handful of whites surrounded by thousands of Indian warriors?

The idea of a Machiavellian scheme seems scarcely worthy of Winslow, Standish, and Bradford and does not comport with their record otherwise. Three things may be noted: (1) No attack was made on either colony. (2) The Wessagusset Colony, with aid from Standish, did fold up and the men joined the fishing fleet off Maine. (3) Massasoit and his tribal federation seem to have accepted the executions as fully justified.

In an historical address on July 4, 1874, at the 250th Anniversary of the settlement of Weymouth, as Wessagusset was later called, Charles Francis Adams, Jr. stated, "In light of the Virginia experience [massacre] of 1622 and the New England Terror during the war of King Philip [Massasoit's son] in 1676, posterity must concede that the severe course of Myles Standish here in Weymouth in March 1623 was the most truly merciful course."

Speaker Adams was chosen to address the gathering as great grandson of Abigail Smith Adams, a native of Weymouth, who was married to John Adams, second President of the United States.

Friendly relations between the Pilgrims and Indians will be detailed later.

CHIEF MASSASOIT: Sketch of Heroic Bronze Statue on Coles Hill at Plymouth by Frank Hockaday.

Commentary "C"

The Hand that Guided the Pilgrims, Four "Miracles" the "Instrument of God", Indian Relations

The Pilgrims believed, as well they might, that the hand of God was guiding them. Once they had set upon a course, nothing seemed to divert them from their purpose. Time and again they faced crucial decision and did not flinch.

In reviewing the story, it would appear that there were at least four occasions when the welfare of the entire expedition hung in the balance. Each time they made the right choice. But, more than this, some providential factor seemed to make it possible.

Some people call such events "miracles". It is likely the Pilgrims believed they were:

The miracle: Voyage of the *Mayflower* is saved.

The *Mayflower*, overloaded with passengers and provisions, had reached mid-Atlantic. After a stormy session with what must have been a hurricane of sorts, it was discovered that a main beam was bowed and cracked. The crew muttered and the mariners debated the sufficiency of the vessel to complete its voyage.

Was the ship likely to fold up, literally, if they continued? Should the voyage be aborted? If they turned back at that point, the passengers would have been landed at Plymouth, England, defeated, homeless, and bankrupt. Governor Carver intervened. Frank M. Gregg wrote in *Founders of a Nation*:

> *"Master Carver, dignified and patient, again held forth his hand bidding the captain to hear him out: 'We think the vessel can be made whole!'"*

From down in the hold one of the passengers produced a lift screw that he had brought from Holland. The ship's carpenter slowly raised the beam into place and inserted two strong timbers to act as props, and the ship, once more sound, was on her way.

Except for the thoughtfulness of one man in bringing the "screw" along, the voyage of the *Mayflower* might have terminated at mid-ocean or been turned to ignominious failure.

The miracle: Pilgrims "directed" to Plymouth and the Mayflower Compact.

It is not clear whether storms or design kept the *Mayflower* well north of Virginia waters. The navigator appeared to be a competent man, and it was revealed that he had previously visited the Cape Cod area and had a map that showed Plymouth harbor, and the Charles River, named for Prince Charles.

But, when the *Mayflower* made its landfall at Cape Cod, there was apparently a restiveness among the passengers. Most had thought they were going to "northern Virginia", which could have embraced territory as far as the present New York. The company held a patent for settlement in Virginia from the crown.

As a result, the ship turned southward, apparently toward the Hudson River. Shortly it ran into adverse winds that pushed it into the area of dangerous shoals. An abrupt halt was called by the captain who returned the ship to Cape Cod.

The clamor among the passengers grew. More than half of the group were "Strangers" and they made it rather clear that, if settlement were to be made outside Virginia, the patent was void and authority over them non-existent. They proposed to go their own way.

This situation led directly to the drawing of the Mayflower Compact, which will be discussed later, and the ultimate agreement to a democratic government by all concerned. The *Mayflower* proceeded to Cape Cod harbor and then Plymouth.

Did a guiding hand lead them to Cape Cod, and turn them back to that destination when they veered away? Had they gone to Virginia, the American democratic process might have been delayed and the course of history altered.

The miracle: Discovery of Indian seed corn.

On one of the first exploratory expeditions to the new coastline a Mayflower party found a large mound, covered by mats and earth. The men dug into the heap and found a cache of newly harvested maize, or Indian corn.

They took as much with them as they could conveniently carry. A few days later they returned to the area. It was covered by one of the first snows of winter. Without their prior knowledge, they would have passed by the mound with its precious store of corn. They carried away some 40 bushels.

At the moment this may not have appeared of great importance but it was to prove essential in the preservation of the colony. The settlers had only a few garden seeds with them, and little cereal seed. With accustomed foresight, they laid aside most of the corn for spring planting. They also determined to give the Indian owners "full satisfaction" when they met.

Except for the bountiful corn crop the next fall, the colony would certainly have perished. What led them to this mound of corn on almost the last day before winter obliterated it?

The miracle: Locating Plymouth harbor and the town site.

The Pilgrims needed a site for their settlement on deep water so that ships could be loaded and unloaded. They needed an area for a settlement located in such a way that it could be defended. They needed a fresh water supply. They needed cleared fields in which to plant corn. They needed to be near favorable fishing and hunting areas.

And they needed a site for which they would not have to contest with the Indians.

In the midst of a raging and blinding snowstorm that nearly swamped their boat, Pilgrim explorers were virtually driven into the shelter of Plymouth harbor. Here they found precisely the site they needed. It was evident that it had been a village but it was empty— not an Indian to contest for it or pay anything for his interest.

The corn fields were cleared but untilled. A brook was at hand with sweet water and a hill behind provided an ideal site for fortifications. This all was most important, as they had no time at all to clear lands before starting to build against the winter that was upon them. And they could live on the *Mayflower* while shelters and storehouses were being prepared.

What had led them to such a site, ready-made for their needs?

The miracle: Friendly, helpful relations with the Indians.
Other white men had been in trouble almost from the start because traders and colonists had treated the Indians badly, and some of them suffered the revenge of the savage.

Where else than at Plymouth on the American coast could Indians have been found who were both peaceful and willing to accept the White Man as a friend and neighbor?

For some five months there had been minor skirmishes between the settlers and the Indians. And the savages skulked about furtively watching from a distance to see what these pale-faced people were doing and trying to determine what it meant to their welfare.

Occasionally, they could be seen looking down from a hill and making hostile gestures. When tools were left in the woods, they appropriated them. But still the new people seemed to offer them no harm. The reason for the Indian shyness was to appear later.

Then, one day a handsome native walked boldly into the settlement and up to the door of the meeting place where the Pilgrims were considering defense measures.

"Welcome," he said in good English, to the amazement of the colonists. It was Samoset, a young Sachem who had learned English from fishermen he had met in Maine, his native country.

The incident proved a key to their future. Samoset brought Squanto to them, and the latter spoke the language fluently. The story goes that a Captain Hunt, about 1614, had lured a crowd of 20 Indians on board ship to trade and had sailed off to sell them into slavery in Spain. Squanto was among them. So were seven Nausets. No wonder the tribesmen were hostile. The Nausets had killed three Englishmen off a ship not eight months before the Pilgrims came.

There are several stories about Squanto's experiences but, in any event, he got to England where he lived several years in the home of John Slanie, treasurer for the Newfoundland Company. Squanto may have returned to America in one of Slanie's ships because he was met in Newfoundland by a Captain Dermer in 1618, who took him back to the Massachusetts coast.

Now the Pilgrims were to learn why they had happened upon a perfect village site that was uninhabited, why there were fields already cleared for planting of corn, why they had no contest with the natives or payments to make for the land.

Squanto was a member of the Patuxet tribe which had lived on the site of Plymouth. In 1617, while he was away, a plague struck the village and wiped it out to the last man. Squanto returned to find that his people were all dead. He was befriended by Chief Massasoit of the Wampanoag tribe.

Squanto, as Bradford observed, was to become "a special instrument of God for their good beyond their expectations". He taught them where and how to catch fish, how to find game, how to plant and tend their corn. This was highly important that first year.

The soil was "old ground", meaning it had been over-cropped. Squanto taught them to put two or three herring in each hill of corn for fertilizer. He told them how deep to plant and how to tend the corn. None of them had grown corn previously—it was an Indian grain.

Without this knowledge there might have been a meager crop and the second winter could have been worse than the first. With their home supplies now virtually depleted, they were largely dependent on the corn. Further, the improvident Adventurers sent them 35 more settlers—without provisions—on the *Fortune* at the end of November. Here were 35 more mouths to feed. What had been thought an abundant harvest turned into an inadequate granary, and the colonists existed on half rations and what the sea and forest could provide.

Without a good crop of corn, there would have been starvation.

Squanto was to tell them that the Indians feared their "firesticks" which had been used indiscriminately against them by the English, who came to fish, trade, and explore. And they had good reason to suspect that the deadly plague had been brought on the big ships.

It was Squanto and Samoset who were to lead the Indians to trade with their furs, and to allay suspicions. They carried the word of friendship and peace to Massasoit. And they brought him to the negotiations with Governor John Carver that produced the famous treaty of good will and alliance on March 22, 1621.

The Pilgrims had something going for them in these negotiations that they did not realize at the time. Squanto knew that the Narragansett federation was quarrelsome and had frequently bullied, plundered and made war on the Wampanoags. With good success, he urged Massasoit to ally himself with the British, whose muskets—if not their number—were greatly feared by all Indians.

The settlers, in turn, knew that the Wampanoags served as a wonderful buffer against other tribes. And Massasoit, a man of great honor, was to observe the treaty faithfully until his death forty years later.

The treaty also provided for return of the stolen tools by the Indians and the payment to the Pamet Indians by the settlers for the corn that had been appropriated by the Pilgrim explorers when they first landed. Nothing like this had ever happened before to the Indians, and they were greatly impressed with the policy of firmness and fairness with which these men operated.

The story of their dealings was to spread, making trading for furs easier. They did not cheat, rob, or corrupt the Indians. They dealt justly and paid adequately for what they took. And Squanto proved to be both a good interpreter and an able negotiator.

The colonists, and especially the Governor, were held in much esteem. The Indians were to listen to them with respect even when they interceded in behalf of rascals who sought to cheat and plunder them of food and furs.

There was more to these relations. The Pilgrims treated the Indian with dignity and with friendship, respecting his personal as well as property rights and receiving him into their community for special occasions.

The most famous of these, of course, was the first Thanksgiving, when they shared their bounty. And the Indians responded by killing five deer and presenting them to the Governor, Captain Standish, and others.

Their dealings with other tribes were equally correct. When toughness was needed, the Pilgrim fathers could be both brave and stern. When the Narragansetts decided to test them with a hostile threat by sending a great snakeskin wrapped around a bundle of arrows, they sent it back with a protestation of friendship on the one hand and a stuffing of powder and bullets on the other.

The Narragansett chief would not touch it but returned it. Nothing more was heard of the affair.

Edward Winslow in his *Good News from New England* wrote:

The Providence of God ... possessed the hearts of the savages with astonishment and fear of us. Whereas if God had let them loose, they might easily have swallowed us up; scarcely being a handful by comparison to those forces they might have gathered together against us ... Blessed therefore be His name! That hath done so great a thing for us.

If any one of the "miracles" had failed the Pilgrims, the Plymouth Plantation might have been still-born.

Commentary "D"

John Carver, Moses of the Pilgrims—a Re-evaluation of Plymouth's First Governor

One of the great ironies of human experience has been the frequency with which a great leader has wrought mightily but has been denied the privilege of sharing the fruits of his labors.

Moses is the classic example. After leading the Children of Israel out of Egypt and through two score years of privation in the wilderness, Moses died. It remained for Joshua, to whom the mantle fell, to take his people into the Promised Land, conquer and settle it.

But, without Moses, there could have been no Promised Land. And the Old Testament story does not overlook his vast contributions.

The same cannot be said of the literature of the Plymouth Colony. It is something of a mystery that so little is known today of John Carver, first governor of Plymouth, who died just as the colony seemed to have become established.

Some of his activities are lightly sketched, although Bradford does give him a brief, generous mention. But the extent of his leadership in planning, organizing, and financing the Mayflower expedition and establishing the colony against almost crushing odds has not been adequately treated.

It is likely that these things were presumed at the time and attention was always directed to new and pressing problems of the present and immediate future.

Carver's influence has been somewhat obscured in history at least, in part, because of his own humility in failing to attribute to himself his own good works.

Evidence in the Pilgrim writings and reasoned evaluation do give the first governor of Plymouth his rightful place as the determined and intelligent leader of the Pilgrims, yet a gentle, humble man of the people.

If we are to accept the accuracy of the Biblical comparison, then William Bradford was the Joshua of the Plymouth Colony. The mantle of leadership fell to him in April, 1621, and he carried it many years. Because he had the foresight and sense of history to make a record of the crucial events of his time, and identify himself with them, he has received well deserved credit and attention.

It should reflect in no way on his achievements to observe that it was Carver who laid the foundations. Nor should it dim that picture to suggest that some works may have been attributed to Bradford, or left unassigned, that both evidence and reason suggest belong to Carver.

The allusion to Carver as the "Moses of the Pilgrims" appeared most apt, but we were to discover that we were not the first to make such application. Archie Lee Talbot, founder of the Mayflower Descendants, State of Maine, wrote:

John Carver—symbol of America's ideals and beliefs—First Governor of Plymouth Colony and the Moses of the Pilgrims:

Governor John Carver is a symbol of rational personal liberty, and the separation of church and state in America. Plymouth Rock is the cornerstone of the Republic.

John Carver was the leader of the God-loving Pilgrim band of exile separatists and our beloved father and founder.

May we digress a moment to observe that certain aberrations have recently appeared in relation to the separation of church and state. These have caused certain people to seek to drive God out of our public life. The men who originated the doctrine of the separation of church and state had no purpose of dispensing with God. They were seeking freedom **of** religion and not freedom **from** religion.

They were fleeing from a state church, monopolistic, compulsory, and corrupt. God, as distinguished from the church, has been from the beginning and is a part of the fabric of all our institutions.

Who was John Carver? He was not a simple tradesman, as were many of the company. He was a man of background and substance. He gave up much, as we learn from this excerpt from George B. Cheever's *Journal of the Pilgrims*:

Truth crushed to earth shall rise again; the eternal years of God are hers.

There would have been no Mayflower Pilgrims but for John Carver who was the leader of the movement in Leyden, Holland, to come to America. Born in Nottinghamshire, England, about 1576, he spent his early life in business, moving to London about 1603 where he acquired in trade what for those days was a considerable fortune. Emigrating to Holland in 1609, he joined the Pilgrims at Leyden, probably in 1610-11. His high character, his stern piety, his maturity (most of them were young men) gave him a place at once among the leaders of the Leyden congregation and he soon was made a deacon of the church; his financial ability enabled him to finance the congregation in part at least and explains, perhaps the purchase of the 'Great House' in which his brother-in-law Reverend John Robinson, their pastor, lived and in which the congregation worshipped, [until invited by the Dutch to share a local sanctuary.]

When the project for emigration to America was formed, Carver and Robert Cushman, also a member of the Leyden group, were sent to England in September, 1617, as agents and organizers to secure permission from the Virginia company to settle their territory. This mission failed [because of the freedom of religion issue], and he then induced London merchants to finance the Plymouth venture, under agreement called Common Stock under which the Pilgrims sailed.

(Later research indicates that John Carver was born in Doncaster, Yorkshire, on the river Don, son of James Carver, yeoman, in 1565, being baptised September 9 of that year.—*Carvers of New England* by Clifford Nickels Carver.)

He hired the Mayflower and he sailed on her July 15, 1620, from London to meet the Speedwell with the Leyden contingent at Southhampton. His wife, Catherine, sailed with him and one of his servants, John Howland, was 13th of the 41 signers of the Mayflower Compact. On board ship John Carver was elected governor and was certainly the mainstay of the Pilgrims. An independent government was formed known as the Compact, drawn and signed in the cabin of the Mayflower by the adult male Pilgrims – in all 41 – the first constitutional government in America.

[Carver was reelected governor March 23, 1621]

Governor Carver was one of the third exploring party to spy out the land and make a choice for settlement of the Pilgrims when in that terrible gale of wind and sleet all came near being lost.

In the great sickness when half their number died, Carver was active and tireless in attendance of nursing the sick.

Nathaniel Morton, for many years secretary of the Plymouth Colony, adds this appraisal:

In the month of April their Governor, Mr. John Carver, fell sick and within a few days he died (he had been in the field when planting seed and became ill, it being a hot day). His death was much lamented and caused great heaviness among them and there was indeed great cause.

This worthy gentleman was one of singular piety and rare humility as appeared by his great condescendency when as these poor people were in great sickness and weakness he shunned not to do every mean service for them, yea for the meanest of them. He bore a share likewise of their labor in his own person, according to their extreme necessity required, who being one of a considerable estate spent the main part of it in this enterprise and from first to last approved himself not only as their agent in the first transacting of things but also all along in the period of his life to be pious, faithful and a very beneficial instrument and now is reaping the fruit of his labors of love with the Lord.

It was the wisdom that comes from God that inspired Governor John Carver to embrace Massasoit and treat him as an equal. Last official act made sacred by the seal of death.

One who visits Coles' Hill in Plymouth may be impressed that there is an heroic statue in bronze of Massasoit. There is none of John Carver, who made the sacred treaty.

In John Goodwin's *Pilgrim Republic*, Chapter XII, (1920), we find:

Governor Carver was not a man to send his associates to duty, but rather to lead them to it; and this day he headed the workers in the field. Their devoted leader had exerted himself incessantly in procuring the outfit of the colony, and in reducing matters to a system, during and after the voyage.

Since then, his cares had been intense, and also his physical efforts. In the landing and building operations; in the long sickness, when for much of the time he had been one of Standish and Brewster's five associates in nursing the cabins full of sick and performing the arduous labors required; from the kitchen and laundry, to the hospital and grave by night and by day—he had been one of these devoted brothers of mercy; in council he had been laborious, and in leadership self-sacrificing and chivalrous. He had used his fair estate for the public good and it was now to be seen that he had also exposed his truly noble life.

He came from the cornfield this (warm) day in April complaining of great pain in his head; he soon became insensible and some days later ceased to breathe. The settlers were overwhelmed with grief at this most unexpected loss; but they bore their leader to Coles' Hill with a truly English regard for official dignity, surrounding the funeral with some small ceremony, and firing volleys of musketry over the unmarked grave.

Before summer had come, that sacred soil was again laid open and the broken-hearted Catherine was laid beside her husband. Almost of them might Elder Brewster have said: 'Lovely and pleasant in their lives, in their death they were not divided'. Of Carver's history no more survives than has been given. Most reluctantly do we turn from the scanty page, which a few strokes of Bradford's pen might have made so luminous.

It may be noted that we have spelled "Catherine" with a "C". Bradford spelled it with a "K", and it so appears in two forms (Katherine, Katharine) on the Plymouth markers. However, Edward Arber reports in his *Story of the Pilgrim Fathers* that her name was on a public record in Leyden as a marriage witness and it appeared "Catherine". We have followed that spelling.

Most authority accepts the idea that Catherine was the sister to Pastor Robinson's wife, Bridget. Goodwin also speculates that they were from a wellplaced family.

Robinson in his farewell letter at the sailing of the *Mayflower* addressed Carver as " brother" in a manner, Goodwin suggests, that seemed to "savor of something more than mere church fraternity". And Robinson mentioned Mrs. Carver as "your good wife, my loving sister".

In Doctor's Commons, London, W. T. Davis found the will of Bishop John White, dated 1621. In it he alluded to a son, not called by name, who had left his country and his church. Davis suggested that Bishop White's son may have been William White of the Mayflower who died in the great illness.

Goodwin in *Pilgrim Republic* further speculates that William was a near kinsman of Roger White of the Leyden colony, brother of Mrs. Robinson and Mrs. Carver. The logic of this would be that they were probably cousins, since they were of similar age.

If so, Mrs. Carver was the niece of a bishop. Such were the times and the deep religious divisions, even within families.

The great man knew not that he was great. It took a century or more for the fact to appear. What he did, he did because he must. It was the most natural thing in the world and grew out of the circumstances of the moment."
                    Ralph Waldo Emerson in *Spiritual Laws*

(It was in the Mayflower Society House that Ralph Waldo Emerson was married to Lydian Jackson in 1835. The house was built in 1754 by Edward Winslow, great-grandson of Pilgrim Edward Winslow. It later came into possession of the Jackson family. In 1941 it was purchased by the General Society of Mayflower Descendants. On the grounds is a small building which houses the library and records for research.)

Commentary "E"

Reweaving tangled threads of History—Who wrote *Journal of the Pilgrims*?—The case for John Carver.

Literature of the Pilgrims began in 1622 with a book known by the improbable title of *Mourt's Relation*. It was almost a day by day diary of the difficulties and bitter hardships of the Plymouth colony through the first winter on the New England coast.

The book was issued by George Morton, who was married to the sister of the second Mrs. William Bradford. In 1848 George B. Cheever re-printed it under the more accurate title of *Journal of the Pilgrims*.

Issuance of the original book by Morton was a fortunate event. But Morton was neither assiduous nor helpful in establishing the authorship of the diary. He merely said:

These relations coming to my hand from my both known and faithful friends on whose writing I do much rely, I thought it not amiss to make them more general, hoping of a cheerful proceeding both of Adventurers and Planters.

He then signed the preface "G. Mourt", a pseudonym that gave the book its cryptic title of "Mourt's Relation". Of course, it was not Mourt's relation, except that he arranged for the publication. Why he chose to obscure the author is subject to conjecture.

The manuscript had been delivered to him by Robert Cushman, when the latter returned on the *Fortune* after visiting the colony in December, 1621. Cushman, as we have seen, was regarded somewhat coolly by the colonists because of his unauthorized agreements with the Adventurers. But he continued as their London agent and eventually won respect, despite what Bradford described as the "infirmities in him".

"After this", said this great historian, "he continued to be a special instrument of their good."

It was evident that Carver differed rather sharply with him over Cushman's early activities. Did Cushman intentionally cover up the authorship? If the writer was Carver, would Cushman have had a motive?

The speculative answer would be, "Yes and no." We are not inclined to entertain seriously the idea that Cushman had a petty reason for suppressing the authorship. Despite the questioning of his judgment on occasion, he was known to have been a man of substance and integrity.

It seems more plausible that *Mourt's Relation* was printed to attract interest in the colony. In fact, Cushman—on reaching home—expressed this desire in a letter saying, "I pray you be advertised a little."

Thus Cushman may have had an understandable motive. As a promotion piece, it might not have had ready acceptance if it had been revealed that the author was the highly respected John Carver and that he, like many others, was dead.

In any event, had the author been Bradford—as many have supposed—would not Morton have had every reason at that, or a subsequent time, to have made the fact clear? After all, Bradford was in the family, as it were.

But, then, we find the same curious characteristic in his son, Nathaniel Morton. The family came to Plymouth on the *Anne* in 1623 when Nathaniel was a small boy. He was a favorite of his uncle and, when George Morton died in 1624, he was brought up in the Bradford home.

He became secretary to the colony in 1645, serving for 40 years. He had full use of Bradford's papers and free communication with John Howland, John Alden and other surviving *Mayflower* passengers. Eventually, from his pen came *New England's Memorial* (1669).

John A. Goodwin in *Pilgrim Republic* (1884) observes of this writing:

A history of the greatest value was therefore to be expected. However, his book is made up of a short series of unskillful abridgements from Bradford. In the absence of Bradford, the abridgement enjoyed a high reputation ... the original writers of high and equal authority have sometimes made contradictory statements.

Nathaniel Morton seems to have occasioned some of them. Like his father, he very largely appropriated the work of another and put it out under his authorship. He did state that he had drawn on his uncle's writings but it was left to Thomas Prince to verify that the "Memorial" was substantially a paraphrase of the Bradford story.

Similarly, Alexander Young made comparisons between a narrative in Nathaniel Morton's own hand, discovered in the library of the Plymouth Church, and extracts from Bradford's manuscript as found in Hutchinson and Prince. He recognized and reported in his *Chronicles of the Pilgrim Fathers* (1841) that the passages were identical with the known parts of Bradford's lost history. In rechecking, Young did find a marginal note achnowledging that the narrative was originally penned by Mr. William Bradford.

But the fact of authorship was unclear and had been overlooked by other historians for more than a century, Nathaniel Morton having been given the credit. When the Bradford manuscript was finally located and copied by permission of the Bishop of London in 1855, it was found that the Morton narrative in the Plymouth Church was a copy of the first nine chapters of that historic document.

Why had Morton failed to credit his uncle properly, either in his *Memorial* or in this narrative? Was it intent or carelessness? Who knows? It seems he had a twinge of conscience when he penned this apologia in his preface to Morton's *Memorial*:

> *Christian Reader:*
> *I have looked at it as a duty incumbent upon me to commit to writing the first beginnings and progress of the church of Christ at Plymouth in New England; forasmuch as I cannot understand that there is anything particularly extant concerning it, and almost all of the members of said church, both elders and others, being deceased by whom intelligence of matters in that behalf might be procured.*

[In 1679, the year previous to the date of the preface, twelve of the original 102 who came over in the *Mayflower* were still living.]

> *I dare not charge the revered elders of that church who are gone to their rest with any neglect on that behalf.*
>
> *... If anything was done on this kind by those worthy leaders, I suppose the blame is rather to be laid on those which had the first view of their studies, and had their books and writings in custody after their decease; for I am persuaded that such was their faithfulness and prudence, as they did not wholly neglect this matter.*

It almost appears he was talking to himself. Young said of him:

> *In fact, Morton's chief merit is that of a diligent, but not always accurate, copyist of his uncle's documents. He would have done a much greater service by causing Governor Bradford's History to be printed entire.*

A further evidence of Morton's lack of historical thoroughness shows in the first line of his *Memorial*, Chapter V:

> *Whereupon two were chosen and sent to England, at the charge of the rest to solicit the matter.*

This was the all-important negotiation between Carver and Cushman, acting for the Pilgrims, and the Adventurers. Any good reporter would have used the names. Why not Morton?

This is an example of how history can be shaped. Somewhere along the line of early historians the suggestion was expressed that Bradford was the author of the *Journal of the Pilgrims*. In view of his prolific writings, this was an easy presumption.

Subsequent writers picked up the assertion, and presumption was built on presumption. Some apparently felt uncertainty and so embellished the idea by suggesting that it was authored by "Bradford and Winslow".

The plain fact is that they did not know and frequent repetition over a long period does not convert conjecture into certainty.

Goodwin in his *Pilgrim Republic* (1884) noted this tendency of writers to repeat unverified information, which he labeled "an apparent neglect to correct, or at least to challenge, the erroneous statements of a far greater number whose historical unreliability is their most remarkable characteristic."

Alexander Young who, as we have observed, did much to pin down the facts of authorship of early documents, noted that George Morton, or "G. Mourt", had no hand in writing the *Journal* but then, in our opinion, fell into the same factual assumption as the rest.

He said, "It was actually written by Bradford and Winslow". Young suggested that many errors had crept into the record and "I have not scrupled to point them out". He added: "For whatever errors I may have fallen into I shall hold myself equally obnoxious to criticism."

Other writers hinted broadly at lapses and errors in the recorded story. Of course, the early writers had to rely on the Mortons and **only** the first nine chapters of Bradford. This was also true of Young.

This may help to explain how, through lack of precise fact, authorship of the *Journal* was assigned to Bradford. Even after the complete manuscript was retrieved, having been lost many years, this assumption persisted—a supposition that appears erroneous on the face of a revealing statement by Bradford from Chapter XI:

Many other smaller matters I omit, sundry of them having been ***already published in a journal made by one of the company****, and some other passages of journeys and relations already published, to which I refer those that are willing to know them more particularly.*

Bradford himself had spoken to the question. The passage had lain dormant until our research brought it to life. The "journal" could not have been other than the *Journal of the Pilgrims* (*Mourt's Relation*) which Bradford had just been paraphrasing. And "one of the company" quite obviously did not mean Bradford himself, otherwise, he would have said "published in my previous journal"—or words to that effect.

We believe evidence and logic point to John Carver as the author of the *Journal of the Pilgrims*. Our reasons:

1. It was the universal custom for the captain of a ship to keep a log. Similarly, the head of a government would see that a record, or diary, of events was kept to demonstrate the manner in which he had discharged his duty. John Carver was the only person to whom the facts were readily accessible and who would have had strong reason to record them.

2. The *Journal of the Pilgrims'* basic narrative began November 9, 1620, two days before Carver was confirmed as governor, as the

Mayflower lay off Provincetown, Cape Cod. It ended March 23, 1621, a few days before Carver's tragic death from sunstroke.

3. William Bradford did not start writing his famous history of the Plymouth colony until 1630 and did not finish it for 20 years. A proud and able man, he did not hesitate to identify himself with his magnificent annals. These represented a recognizable effort to make a record of his own stewardship as long-term governor. In the winter of 1620-21 he was not in a position of leadership and had no pressing reason to record events. It appears unlikely that he would have failed to associate his name with the *Journal*, if he had written it.

4. Bradford virtually disclaimed authorship, saying the *Journal* was "made by one of the company."

5. The style of the *Journal of the Pilgrims* and Bradford's were different. The *Journal* was written mostly in the first person—"we" did this and that. Bradford wrote mostly in the third person—"they" did this and that. Bradford seemed frequently detached. The writer of the *Journal* was directly involved. We believe that the *Journal* was kept by Carver as a diary or log of his term as governor. The *Journal* was direct, its action often crisp. Bradford was inclined to be wordy. The *Journal* wasted few words.

6. Another convincing point indicating Carver's authorship is the use of the personal pronoun "I" at the time of the treaty negotiations with Massasoit: "One thing I forgot, the King had in his bosom hanging by a string a great long knife." Massasoit was seated by the Governor, who was the only one who could have made that observation.

7. What of Edward Winslow? He was a short-time governor of the colony at a later date. He was the known author of *Good News from New England* (1624). He also wrote letters of his journeys to Indian country, which were published with "Mourt". These were identified with his initials "E.W." There appears no adequate reason why he would not have also signed the *Journal* had he written it. His style does not conform to that of the *Journal*.

8. After the treaty was made, Governor Carver conducted King Massasoit to the brook where they embraced and the King departed. Winslow had been sent to invite the king to the parley with Carver and was kept by the king's brother as hostage until

Massasoit was returned to his people. He was not where he could have observed.

Winslow could have been the penman, but we think both logic and evidence point to Carver as the author of the *Journal of the Pilgrims.*

Commentary "F" - Section 1

The Beginning of America: Mayflower Compact, Prototype of the Declaration of Independence and the Constitution of the United States.

Embedded in the *Journal of the Pilgrims* was the text of a covenant which was to determine a steady course for America's future. This was the Mayflower Compact, surely the most significant document of the Pilgrims.

It was the ultimate influence of the Compact on American life and government that led Thomas Carlyle many years later to say of the *Mayflower* landfall at Provincetown:

It was properly the beginning of America. There were struggling settlers in America before ... but the soul of it was this.

Similarly, Bancroft in his United States History characterized the signing of the Compact thus:

This was the birthplace of popular constitutional government.

Before they left England, Pastor John Robinson reminded the Pilgrim band in a letter that they would not have "persons of special eminence", meaning royal governors; that they would be free to choose "such person as so entirely love, and will promote, the common good." This was the simple enunciation of the democratic process—a rule by the consent of the governed. It has been widely regarded as inspiring the Compact.

The Pilgrims needed one thing further, and Robinson added a divine blessing:

"The image of the Lord's power and authority which the magistrate beareth is honourable".

One must understand that the *Mayflower* passengers were not a homogeneous group. Many of them were "strangers" to the Leyden flock. They gave signs of going their own way once a landing was effected. Wise leadership proposed an agreement that should bind them all to submit to "such government and governors as we should by common consent agree to make and choose." (*Journal of the Pilgrims*).

From the MAYFLOWER COMPACT

Signed November 11, 1620, off Provincetown, Cape Cod

We ... having undertaken for the glory of God and advancement of the Christian faith, and honor of our King and Country, a voyage to plant the first colony in the Northern parts of Virginia, do by these presents solemnly and mutually in the presence of God and of one another, covenant, and combine ourselves together into a civil body politic for our better ordering and preservation, and furtherance of the ends aforesaid; and by virtue hereof to enact, constitute, and frame such just and equal laws, ordinances, acts, constitutions, offices from time to time, as shall be thought most meet and convenient for the general good of the colony; unto which we promise all due submission and obedience.

It is not improbable that the rigors of the passage and the unknown dangers of the New England coast sobered the dissidents and made them more willing to join in the Compact. Also, the evident good will of the Leyden contingent in giving them equal status may have impressed them that this was the way to go.

Only with such unity and discipline could the colony have survived in the days just ahead. In all of this, the guiding hand of John Carver appears. Wrote Bradford some ten or more years later:

In these hard and difficult beginnings, they found some discontents and murmurings arise amongst some, and mutinous speeches ... in others, but they were soon quelled and overcome by the wisdom, patience, and just and equal carriage of things by the Governor.

While the words "just and equal" described the "carriage" of the Governor, it is implicit that they were the precepts that Carver must have expressed as well as exemplified. And they were the very words contained in the covenant that followed.

We regard this as highly indicative of the role Carver played both in the shaping and the acceptance of the Compact.

The mutterings were premised on the fact that the landing was being made outside of the Virginia patent granted by the Crown. It was argued that there would be no legally established authority.

Among the "Strangers", however, was Stephen Hopkins, who had been through a similar experience. A ship on which he took passage for Virginia with Governor Gates in 1609 was wrecked at Bermuda. Hopkins, among others, asserted that the company was free of subordination to the Virginia Company. He was accused of treason, but was given a pardon by Gates.

With that background and despite a reputation for occasionally obstinate conduct, he was reported to have counseled the desirability of unity, and he signed the Compact. Others followed, and the crisis passed.

The importance of the Mayflower Compact is indicated in a speech by John Quincy Adams in 1802:

This is perhaps the only instance in human history of that positive, original social compact which speculative philosophers have imagined as the only legitimate source of government.

Here was unanimous and personal assent by all individuals of the community to the association by which they became a nation. The settlers of all the former European colonies had contented themselves with powers conferred upon them by their respective charters without looking beyond the seal of the royal parchment for the measure of their rights and the rule of their duties.

The founders of the Plymouth Colony had been impelled by the peculiarities of their situation to examine their subject with deeper and more comprehensive research.

These were the days when the civilized nations of the world were still ruled by sovereigns with "divine right". It was, therefore, of great significance that this small group should set an example, or pattern, that was to spread through the colonies, as each sought in its own way to attain a greater measure of freedom.

The fact was that the Pilgrims had no other government. The one which they formed was pure democracy, later to be modified and extended. At least one writer has discounted their efforts as "accidental". Hardly. In perspective, it can be seen easily that the Compact was an outgrowth of the Pilgrims' beliefs and bitter experiences.

They had come to the conviction that religion should be a matter of individual conscience and belief. It should be remembered that the King of England was also the head of the church. What was more logical than that they should step from the search for religious freedom to the discovery also of political freedom?

Of course, they were not profound political philosophers. They were realists. They reached for a solution to an unfamiliar situation and found a direct, simple answer. They may not have comprehended fully the logic of their own ideas. But the document was to be precursor of vast political changes both on this continent and in the world.

The Mayflower contingent did not break with the Crown. They were careful to recognize James I as their sovereign. They wanted no trouble on that score. But he was far away. He exercised no control, and for many years the Crown asserted none. They were free to give expression to their aspirations and let them grow.

They did not undertake to set up an entire structure. By "mutual covenant" they did determine that government should rest on the consent of the governed, and they combined themselves into "a civil body politic" for this purpose. In furtherance, they decided to "enact, constitute, and frame such just and equal laws" as thought needed for the "general good of the colony", and to elect such officers as required. The rest was to be evolved.

They probably recorded the desire that was in the hearts of many Englishmen but which had no effective avenue of expression in the old country. Up to that time, the English had made petition for greater liberties "under the crown."

A major breakthrough had come in June, 1215 at a meadow near London called Runnymede. There resolute barons had forced King John to sign an agreement known as Magna Carta, binding the king to uphold certain principles of liberty, social rights and constraints on his power. While the document did not guarantee political or civil rights to the common people, it did set a pattern by which, over intervening centuries, subjects had demanded that the previously absolute monarch grant increasing rights and that, he himself, live by the law.

The Mayflower Compact was a departure from this process. For the first time it placed sovereignty in the people, not a king. It made government the servant and not the master. None had preference before the "just and equal" laws adopted by the majority. This was the spark of a new system, the like of which existed nowhere.

Rose T. Briggs, director emeritus of Pilgrim Hall Museum, writes in the book *They Knew They Were Pilgrims*:

> In 1636 the General Court of Plymouth Colony recorded that having read the Compact and the Letters of Patent of 1629 and finding that 'as freeborn subjects of the State of England we came here endowed with all privileges belonging to such, we think good that it be established as an act ... no imposition, law or ordinance be made or imposed upon us by ourselves or others at present or to come, but such as shall be made by consent, and no otherwise.'
> Neither John Adams nor John Hancock said it better.

Mere accident? The evidence is clear that the Pilgrims knew what they were doing, and what they were doing was to become the American way. Government by consent, the foundation of the democratic system.

Some 156 years later Thomas Jefferson was to pen the charter of American freedom which proclaimed:

> We hold these truths to be self-evident, that all men are created equal, that they are endowed by their Creator with certain unalienable Rights, that among these are Life, Liberty and the pursuit of Happiness.

It was a moral truth beyond need for demonstration, but it

was the unmistakable rhetorical restatement and elaboration of the "just and equal laws" of the Mayflower Compact.

In this modern day it is difficult to realize the injustice and the inequalities of a structured society, with nobility and aristocracy at the top. Class and privilege had been the order of things socially, economically and politically. The average person had little and could aspire to little more.

The laws were framed to keep him in his place, and he had almost no voice in the way he was governed except that which a rudely expressed public opinion could bring to bear. The few men who lifted their heads above the crowd to assert the rights of the many were promptly struck down.

And it had been the same in the church. The Pilgrims established democracy in religion—the right of each man to decide by his own conscience how he would worship God. The Compact gave each man the right to participate in enactment of the laws and assured him of "just and equal" treatment.

Some 3000 miles from the seat of power, they were free to establish a new society in which rights, including the rights of property, were equal. Free to survive, if they could. They began with little except a will to achieve, an overriding respect for the rights of their fellows and their own frail physical force, a most significant break with the past. And survive they did, one of the great examples of courage and fortitude in human history.

A century and a half later these beginnings bore fruit in the determination of the thirteen colonies to enjoy the human freedom for which the Pilgrims yearned and for which they staked their all. Many factors contributed to this growth, but first came the seed!

"Life, liberty and property!" the "Sons of Liberty" chanted under the "Liberty Trees" that were set up in various colonies. In this day the question has sometimes been raised about "human rights over property rights". These men knew instinctively the "property rights" were "human rights".

Nevertheless, Jefferson was to give the slogan a broader application: "Life, liberty and the pursuit of happiness". Owning one's own land and his own home, enjoying the fruits of his own labor and of freedom from suppression and harassment—these things were implicit in the "pursuit of happiness". And the colonies gladly adopted the phrase.

The Compact was known to have been a pattern for other written governmental covenants in New England. Its impact and the Pilgrim example gradually softened the restrictive, arbitrary, and intolerant society of Massachusetts Bay Colony. By the time the more free and tolerant Plymouth Colony was absorbed into Massachusetts Bay Colony in 1692 the latter was ready to open privileges to all.

Massachusetts Bay, in years ahead, was to become a focal point of agitation for free and equal rights.

It is possible to trace physically the spread of the democratic ideal to other colonies. Ideas that are worthy tend to be appropriated by others and become common property. Jefferson is quoted as saying that ideas were "of all things in nature the least capable of confinement or exclusive appropriation".

In writing the Declaration of Independence, Jefferson said he did not seek to state "new principles or new arguments, never before thought of" but to give expression to the "American mind".

Serving with Jefferson on the drafting committee was John Adams of Massachusetts. Adams has generally been credited with having been the ablest advocate of the Declaration of Independence in the Continental Congress.

As a matter of fact, there is little doubt that he was largely responsible for shaping the climate in the colonies, and especially in Congress, for such a declaration. He was likewise influential in determining its content.

Jefferson was a master of words. Adams was master of meanings. Realizing his influence, Jefferson requested Adams to draw the Declaration. Adams declined. He had prodded Congressional members, especially those from Pennsylvania and New York, so hard that he felt certain they would not welcome a document written by him—and unanimity was required.

An author from Virginia was ideal and so was Jefferson, a man facile of expression. Adams was certain Jefferson could write a document to which the colonies would subscribe and for which the world would have comprehension and approval. He told the reluctant Jefferson:

"You can write ten times better than I can."

A third member of the drafting committee was Benjamin Franklin, but he was distracted by an attack of gout. Two other members, Robert Livingston and Roger Sherman, seem to have offered little but encouragement.

But Adams supplied ideas. Jefferson supplied ringing phrases. Franklin, a master of epigram, did the editing of Jefferson's draft. Thus, Jefferson wrote, "We hold these truths to be sacred and undeniable". Franklin struck out "sacred and undeniable" and wrote in the simple, direct "self-evident".

Adams was insistent in one regard. He believed that the "law of nature" meant God's law by which man is born to liberty. This was also a doctrine expounded by John Locke in England a century before and Adams found in it an exposition of his own philosophy. He wanted it included.

"I was very strenuous for retaining and insisting on the Law of Nature", Adams wrote.

And so Jefferson began the Declaration:

"When in the course of human events it becomes necessary for one people to dissolve the political bonds which have connected them with another, and to assume among the powers of the earth the separate and equal station to which the laws of nature and of nature's God entitle them, a decent respect to the opinions of mankind requires that they should declare the causes which impel them to the separation."

There followed a bill of particulars against the Mother Country, including intolerable taxes, economic suppression, violations of fundamental rights.

John Adams wrote his wife, Abigail, "Great Britain has at last driven America to the last step."

Adams carried the parliamentary action for the Declaration on the floor of the Continental Congress, meeting in Philadelphia, just as he had stood staunchly and sometimes alone for the cause of freedom over the past months. Many colonists and members of Congress had hoped for reconciliation with England.

But now King George III, a sometimes irrational monarch, had himself blocked such efforts. He had declared the colonies to be in a state of insurrection. He had blockaded the coastline. He had hired Hessian mercenaries to reinforce his armies and put down the rebellion. General Howe, forced out of Boston by colonial militiamen under George Washington, had reformed his forces and was bearing down on New York with an armed flotilla and transports filled with "Redcoats".

The situation was grim. Adams, on July 1, laid out the facts in measured terms and offered the Declaration of Independence as the only suitable response.

Resistance, which had been prolonged, skillful and often emotional, suddenly crumbled under the force of Adams' words and logic. No record of the talk was kept and Adams later could not reconstruct it except for the introduction:

"Every honest person with an open mind and senses alert can hear the moment strike for action, knows when the path turns beneath his feet... ."

Jefferson, years after, was to write, "He came out with a power of thought and expression that moved us from our seats."

Members of Congress knew that Adams was right. The moment for action had struck. The vote on July 2 was 12 colonies in the affirmative for the Resolution of Independence. New York delegation, lacking instructions, delayed and added its vote later.

Adoption of the formal Declaration of Independence came on July 4, 1776. It was read to the public at Independence Hall in Philadelphia, July 8. There was little celebration at that time. Listeners accepted the text with deep feeling and went soberly to their appointed tasks. Five years of bitter and difficult fighting, and sacrifices, lay ahead before General Washington was to accept the surrender of Cornwallis at Yorktown.

"I am well aware," wrote Adams to his wife, "of the toil and blood and treasure it will cost us to maintain this Declaration and support and defend these states. Yet, through all gloom, I can see the rays of ravishing light and glory."

Action by Congress actually spanned three days. Adams wanted the occasion to be remembered as a "Day of Deliverance by solemn acts of devotion to God Almighty." He predicted that "posterity will triumph in that day's transaction."

Jefferson and Adams, who had merged their differing personalities to produce the Declaration, drifted into separate political factions. Adams defeated Jefferson for vice-president under Washington. Then Jefferson defeated Adams for reelection to his second presidential term.

For a time they were estranged but were reconciled and corresponded in their later years, as Adams said "to explain ourselves to each other."

This correspondence was applauded by Dr. Benjamin Rush, a member of the Continental Congress and a signer of the Declaration of Independence. In one of a series of letters to Adams he said:

I hope the chain which now connects Quincy with Monticello continues to brighten by every post.

He went on to illuminate the roles played by Adams and Jefferson in a letter dated February 17, 1812:

I rejoice in the correspondence which has taken place between you and your old friend, Mr. Jefferson. I consider you and him as the North and South poles of the American Revolution. Some talked, some wrote and some fought to promote and establish it, but you and Mr. Jefferson thought for us all.

On July 4, 1826—the 50th anniversary of adoption of the Declaration of Independence—Adams lay dying at Braintree (Quincy). It was his 90th year. He roused himself and, in a last dramatic recognition and tribute to the "trumpeter of freedom", murmured:

"Thomas Jefferson still lives!"

He was mistaken, Jefferson died earlier that very day in Virginia.

But, in a larger sense, Thomas Jefferson did live on in his immortal work.

And how do we connect the Mayflower compact with this? The Compact was part of John Adams' heritage. Adams was born and reared at Braintree, which was on the road between Boston and Plymouth. His grandmother was Hannah Bass Adams, a granddaughter of John and Priscilla Alden of Mayflower fame.

John had many close connections with Plymouth and practiced law in the Plymouth Courthouse. It is recorded of Adams that he was faithful to his beginnings—"their signature lay upon him to the end."

More than most Americans know, Adams was also influential in shaping the governments of various colonies. He was asked by members of Congress what form of government he would advise. He responded:

A plan as nearly resembling the government under which we were born and have lived, as circumstances in the country will admit.

He pointed out that they had had no kings, nobles or hereditary positions. He suggested governors, legislatures, councils and judges should be chosen "by elections".

And so he envisaged a "civil body politic" that would be the servant and not the master of its citizens. There would be no men of position except those elected by the people. Men would be equal under the law. This was the embryo system created under the Mayflower Compact.

North Carolina Provincial Assembly formally instructed its delegates to "apply to Mr. Adams for his views on the form of government they should assume if independence be declared." And so Adams set down "A Plan" which he eventually sent to Virginia, New Hampshire, North Carolina and New Jersey.

All of this was months before the Declaration of Independence, and helped to shape the "American mind", which Jefferson undertook to interpret and which the framers of the Constitution undertook to implement. The spiritual concept of the democratic system, implicit in the aspirations of the Pilgrims, had become the guiding principle of a new nation.

Plymouth has an even more intimate claim to inspiring the Independence movement, again pointing to the heritage handed down from the Mayflower Compact. Boston is rightfully credited with many dramatic incidents that preceded the Revolution. What is not generally known, or appreciated, is that much of the planning for this resistance to suppressive controls of the British Crown was centered in Plymouth.

Three of the early leaders of the movement were James Otis, James Warren and Mrs. James Warren, who was Mercy Otis, sister of James Otis. The Plymouth mansion of the Warrens is credited in some historical works as the "breeding place of the American

Revolution." Numerous meetings were held there and the philosophy and tactics of liberty-minded colonists evolved.

James Otis was a practicing attorney in Plymouth until he became King's Advocate in Boston. This position he resigned in 1760 when the Writs of Assistance were promulgated by Britain. The writs authorized inspection of any shop or building at will by customs officials seeking untaxed goods.

Otis undertook the defense of 60 merchants who resisted the writs. Before a court of five justices, convened in the Old State House, James Otis in stentorian tones proclaimed:

Taxation without representation is tyranny!

It was to become the rallying cry of the Revolution.

John Adams, a close friend, was in court that day and heard the pronouncement. He later wrote:

"Then and there, the child Independence was born."

Otis and Mercy, his sister, were raised in a family of 13 children on a farm at Barnstable, Cape Cod. Plymouth was their cultural center. Their mother was a descendant of a signer of the Mayflower Compact, Edward Doty. Otis was to set up law practice in "town" and Mercy was to marry James Warren, successful merchant-farmer and descendant of Richard Warren, also a signer of the Mayflower Compact. Brother and sister were close and shared many opinions. The Warren home became the center for lively political discourse.

At first, Otis held to the idea that colonial status under the king, with parliamentary representation, was the best plan. Gradually he came to the conviction that the only way the colonists could become masters of their own destinies was to sever relations with a capricious monarch. He was a natural leader for budding revolutionaries.

After his powerful plea before the court, the judges failed to rule. But the writs were little used thereafter in the Boston area. Otis had made his point—"an act against natural equity is void."

Equal rights under the law: Words of the Mayflower Compact were echoing down the corridors of time!

Otis' legal skills and ideas were widely acclaimed. He became a member of the Massachusetts House of Representatives and met regularly with Samuel Adams, Paul Revere, John Hancock, Joseph

Warren and Benjamin Church. He carried on a vigorous schedule, meeting, speaking and writing.

Mercy Otis Warren was his counterpart, welcoming revolutionaries to her Plymouth home. The Stamp Act demonstrations of 1765, and others, were said to have been planned there.

Mercy Warren and Abigail Adams were constantly in touch. In Braintree, Abigail found herself, like Mercy, center of lively controversy. Neighbors came with questions. Not only was she wife of John Adams, delegate to Congress, but she was a Quincy by her own right. Her house was on the Boston-Plymouth highway and it was a stopping place for many who shared the American dream. Even Dr. Benjamin Franklin and General and Mrs. George Washington visited there.

James Warren served as a member of the Massachusetts House and corresponded regularly with John Adams while the latter was in Philadelphia at the historic sessions of the Continental Congress. At the death of General Joseph Warren at Bunker Hill, James Warren succeeded him as president of the Congress of the Province. Again it may be seen that Plymouth's influence and traditions helped to shape early America, despite its limited size.

The warm attitude of the Adams family toward the Mayflower Compact was reflected in the remarks of John Quincy Adams, son of John, previously quoted. John Adams was the second President of the United States. John Quincy Adams was the sixth—the only father and son combination in the annals of the presidency.

It ought to be amply clear that John Quincy Adams drew his ideas on the Compact from the same fountain-head as that from which flowed inspiration for the Declaration of Independence and the American Consitution.

John Adams may not have identified the Mayflower Compact in his writings as the start of a new system and the departure from the monarchial pattern of government, as John Quincy Adams had done, but he came very close to it. Adams, in his extensive correspondence in his later years with Dr. Benjamin Rush, wrote in a letter dated May 23, 1807:

The claim of the 1776 men to the honor of first concieving the idea of American Independence or of first inventing the project of it is as ridiculous as that of Dr. Priestly to discovery of the perfectibility of man. I hereby disclaim all pretensions to it because it was much more ancient than my nativity.

Regarding adoption of the Declaration, Hannah Arendt observed: *"One of the rare moments in history when the power is great enough to erect its own monument."*

The same could be said with equal verity regarding the signing of the Mayflower Compact.

The Compact established a democratic system apart from the Crown but with tenuous relations to it. The Declaration of Independence severed those ties. The Constitution formalized the democratic system into government structure.

As the Declaration followed the Compact, so the Constitution came from the Declaration—a codification of the revered principle of democracy, the worth and dignity of the individual. It also appointed his privileges and his duties.

And, so, reviewing the sweep of history, we join Carlyle in characterizing that moment of truth in the Mayflower cabin—the Pilgrim settlers pledging their faith in a democratic system—as the real "beginning of America".

> *As one small candle may light a thousand, so the light here kindled hath shone unto many, yea in some sort to our whole nation.*
>
> William Bradford

Commentary "F" - Section II

To Secure the Blessings of Liberty—The American Revolution

Unlike any major revolution in history, the American war for independence did not seek to overthrow social and political systems. It sought to preserve them.

The French, who toppled the monarchy, went on to throw out several other regimes before settling on their present form of government. By contrast, the American version was a "law and order" revolution. The French called it "incomplete".

What they did not realize was that the American Revolution had been in progress for 170 years. John Adams, who served as a philosophical bridge between colonial beginnings and the spirit of the new republic, acknowledged this in a letter saying that the American Revolution began in 1620 at the landing of the Pilgrims at Plymouth.

In other letters, Adams had repeatedly asserted that the Revolution was not an instant political upheaval but a process of long growth, not a rebellion against a system but a revolution against a King who was thwarting the process and progress of a free society that the colonists were evolving and already enjoying to a great extent.

In the year 1775, as the revolutionary clouds were gathering, Edmund Burke evidenced both his understanding and friendship for America by telling the English Parliament:

The colonies in general owe little or nothing to any care of ours ... but through a wiser and salutary neglect a generous nature has been suffered to take her own way to perfection.

In a recent monograph, Irving Kristol, educator and political philosopher, took note of the early origins of independent democratic thought and reminded his readers:

The primordial American 'social contract' was signed and sealed on the Mayflower—literally signed and sealed. The subsequent signatures appended to the Declaration of Independence, beginning with John Hancock's, are but an echo of the original covenant.

Far from rebelling against the social order, the states of the fledgling nation moved at once to adopt constitutions which confirmed and extended it, especially in the area of local self-government. Kristol lamented that "we have forgotten our revolutionary heritage" and added:

Our revolutionary message—which is a message not of the Revolution itself but of the American political tradition from the Mayflower to the Declaration of Independence to the Constitution—is that a self-disciplined people can create a political community in which an ordered liberty will promote both economic prosperity and political participation.

It was natural that the new states should think first of their own governance, and recoil from a strong central government, but gradually they came to recognize that they must eventually think in national terms.

The colonies had enjoyed long years of freedom and had resisted efforts of the Crown to assert control. This resistance to central control was also reflected in the very loose relationship under which they prosecuted the war. The Continental Congress did attempt to make decisions, levy on the colonies for men, materiel and money, but the states were free to comply or reject all or any requests.

At times General George Washington was more heavily engaged with trying to obtain support for his rag-tag army than he was with the enemy. The play "1776" dramatized this anomaly by having Washington write to the Congress when he failed to get funds to pay and supply his men:

Is anybody there? Does anybody care?

During the first two years of the war, the Continental Congress was really little more than a supreme war council for the separate colonies, which were allied but fiercely independent. Then the Articles of Confederation were drafted in 1777 to legalize the situation. The states were slow to ratify and Maryland, the last, gave approval in 1781. The Articles brought small improvement, with the states continuing to exercise control over taxation, commerce and customs.

But, Washington managed to hold his army together by force of character and, with timely aid from the French, he struggled on to victory. Although flushed by the improbable military success, the Confederation barely functioned. It was authorized to make war and peace, conduct foreign affairs, control the currency, borrow money, settle boundary disputes and made treaties with the Indians. But the states, as sovereign entities, retained the real powers to govern and tax within their boundaries.

The Articles were flawed from the outset, as each state went its own way. The Congress wrestled with its weaknesses, often futilely, while the conviction grew among influential men that a stronger union was essential. Still resistance persisted.

The citizens of Ashfield, Massachusetts, resolved, "We do not want any goviner but the Goviner of the Universe." It was a common sentiment.

The one inevitable result of the Confederation experiment was to prove what would not work. Domestic affairs drifted. While foreign governments respected such emissaries as Benjamin Franklin, John Adams and Thomas Jefferson, it was evident that they considered the new American nation to be weak and ineffective, despite its good intentions. Was this the fruit of the democratic way?

George Washington, from his retirement home in Mount Vernon, Virginia, wrote that he wondered if the Revolution had been worth the cost in sacrifice and blood. He continued:

We are either a united people under one head for federal purposes, or we are thirteen independent sovereignties, eternally counteracting each other.

Reluctantly, the states agreed to a meeting in May, 1787 at Philadelphia to "amend" the Articles. Fifty-five delegates responded and, while they asserted the same suspicions and differences as the states from which they came, they were able to agree that only a representative republic, responsible to the people, could fulfill the promise of the Revolution.

Despite lack of authority, they convened themselves into a constitutional convention, scrapped the Articles and began to discuss a new plan of government. Those who composed the gathering proved to be men of remarkable fitness for their task, not the least of which was facility at constructive compromise—ability to overcome implacable differences.

At this juncture, James Madison, a scrupulous student of political science, came foreward with a plan to combine effective government with protection for personal liberty. He conceived a system of "checks and balances" between three branches of government—executive, legislative and judicial. It constituted the framework of the new political structure that was to come.

The biggest roadblock to the sessions arose over representation. The big states wanted representation in the legislative branch to be apportioned according to population. The little states wanted it to be by states only, each having an actual vote. The "great compromise" provided for division of the Congress into two houses. The House of Representatives would consist of members elected to the body from districts in the states, the numerical representation being based on population. The Senate would consist of two members from each state, elected by the several legislatures.

(This latter provision was to persist into the present century before adoption of the 17th Amendment provided direct election of senators.)

Once that hurdle was surmounted, the delegates more readily agreed to give Congress the power to regulate commerce, raise money by taxation, borrow on the national credit and coin money and regulate its value.

But, creation of an executive posed problems. Some wanted a committee rather than a single person, in order to avoid creating a monarch. James Wilson, noted for his lectures on law at the University of Pennsylvania and afterwards a member of the Supreme Court, spoke out strongly for a single executive, arguing that he could function more decisively and responsibly than a committee. The convention followed his lead.

Similarly, Wilson prevailed on the method of choosing the executive. A strong faction wanted the president to be elected by the Congress. Wilson persuaded them that only a president elected by the people could have the broad acceptance needed to govern.

Through three and a half months of often strenuous debates, members labored until a new instrument of government was articulated. Gouverneur Morris was assigned the duty of drafting the new constitution into precise and impressive English. On September 17, 1787, forty-two delegates signed the document. The first states ratified speedily but others hung back, and it was two and a half years before all had signed.

John Adams characterized the convention as the "greatest single effort of national deliberation that the world has seen."

William Gladstone, British statesman, also reached for superlatives, saying the Constitution was "the most wonderful work ever struck off at a given time by the brain and purpose of man."

A document of great worth had been brought into being—the first written constitution of a democratic republic and one of such merit that it was to endure for two centuries virtually unchanged in basic form.

It was a nobler effort than even the framers themselves realized, a great source of American pride, faith and reverence.

Wilson, the legal scholar and the one credited by many authorities with being, next to Madison, perhaps the most influential in shaping the federal Constitution, gave one of several lectures in 1790, outlining the work of the convention. The audience was a blue ribbon one, including President and Mrs. Washington.

Law, he said, must be studied as historical science and, in this light, stories of the early colonies were imperfectly known, their histories yet to be written. In his search for the origin of principles that shaped American democratic aspiration, he revealed, he had come upon a document in *Chalmers Political Annals*. He would read it to them.

"I shall have the pleasure of presenting to my hearers," he said with evident satisfaction, "what must be searched for in vain—an original compact of a society on its first arrival in this section of the globe."

What he read was the Mayflower Compact. His lecture effectively placed the birthplace of American constitutional government on the Mayflower.

And thus, from the vantage of a century plus seventy years, inspired men had formed another, more mature, "civil body politic"—the United States of America.

"Out of the Mayflower Compact came as naturally as comes the oak from the acorn, the Declaration of Independence and the Constitution of the United States ..."

Dr. Raymond B. Walker, Distinguished Congregational
Church minister and student of Pilgrim History.

Commentary "G"

Authors of our Heritage: The Pilgrims and their Dream

The Pilgrims initiated an heroic philosophy and brought it to our shores. They were willing to stake their possessions and their lives to build something new.

These aspirations were carried over into the motivation of American pioneers, who pushed ever to the West to find new homes and found new commonwealths. In the process they, too, left behind comforts, friends and positions.

It was more than a quest for fortune. It was a lure of new lands, new opportunities, and a chance to erect new foundations.

The story of the Pilgrim Fathers well exemplifies the Providential law which evolves good out of evil. They had a character born of high spiritual values and hardship. And they lived the kind of moral lives in which they believed.

Thus, the "Dutch would trust them in any reasonable matter when they needed money." They were careful to keep their word and they refused even to repudiate the debts which were loaded on them cruelly by rascals. They were "painful and diligent in their callings."

In Leyden the magistrates were to say that for 12 years "we have never had a suit or accusation come against them".

In an age when doctrines of tolerance were unknown, they were thrust forth from their native land on account of their religious beliefs and compelled to carry them to the New World.

Although they were possessed of humility and were devoid of ostentation, it should in nowise be presumed that they were weak.

They were steadfast in face of the greatest odds and obstacles. Even though half the colony died of the great illness, probably a virulent influenza, complicated by scurvy, during the first winter, not a man returned to England when the *Mayflower* sailed in April, 1621!

Theirs is a story of abiding faith in God, His plan for them and His leadership. It is a story of deep conviction. They knew it meant their lives if they were wrong. But they were determined on democratic procedures, freedom of thought, speech, conscience, freedom to worship as they pleased.

In *Pilgrim Republic* Goodwin characterized them:

They were great in their goodness and wise beyond their generation. In an era of superstition, they groped for something better. They bequeathed to their successors the spirit of inquiry and progress.

They were likewise influential far beyond their numbers. We see this emerge during the voyage of the *Mayflower*, in the signing of the Compact, in the first months of the settlement.

Of the party of 102 on board the Mayflower only 40, including 14 children, were of the Leyden congregation. The rest were "Strangers" sent over by the Merchant Adventurers. At the end of the winter only 20 Leyden folk had survived sickness.

Only 18 of those men who had signed the Compact were living, and only six of these were "Saints" from Leyden. And yet this little group remained the dominant influence in affairs of the colony. Its bearing was such that it drew to itself staunch men from ranks of the Strangers.

Two of the better known are Myles Standish and John Alden. Standish was a soldier of fortune. He signed on to the expedition to head up its defense forces, such as they were. John Alden was a cooper. He needed a job. He was hired to build and repair barrels and casks required for storage of food and beverages. Both became solid members of the colony. Others did likewise.

Said Bradford Smith in his *Bradford of Plymouth*:

Here [in Plymouth] originate ... outright ownership of land, rather than the feudal types of tenure, a classless society, in an age of rigid class distinctions, and government by free association of the governed.

The Pilgrims proved that a community of families could survive in the New World and it could live at peace with the surrounding

Indians. Out of Plymouth came a system of government—the town meeting—which colored and enriched the bloodstream of American democracy.

Boston and Massachusetts, Smith said, "tried to reestablish place and privilege as they had known them in England." The Pilgrims in the New World strove to make men free and equal. Although the Massachusetts Bay Colony was much the larger, the Plymouth ideal ultimately prevailed.

A corollary fact, apparently little noted, was that the colony was "integrated". Abraham Peirce came on the *Anne* in July, 1623. Goodwin in *Pilgrim Republic* reported that he was "for many years the only Negro at Plymouth, and was an energetic citizen of Duxbury, both in matters of peace and war."

Peirce's employer may have been the master of the *Anne*, and from him he derived his name. At a town meeting June 1, 1627, Peirce was a member of a Company of 12 which drew the third lot entitling them jointly to a red cow with a bull calf. Eight months later he sold his interest to Myles Standish for two ewe lambs, the first intimation that there were sheep in the colony.

John Pory, secretary of the Virginia Colony, on a visit to Plymouth, gave his opinion, it will be recalled, that the colony set an example for others.

Sir Thomas Hutchinson, Tory governor of the Bay Colony, whose aristocratic tastes were well known and who was not otherwise given to undue estimation of the "uncourtly and unchartered" settlers at Plymouth, nevertheless wrote in his history:

These were the founders of the Colony of New Plymouth. The settlement of this Colony occasioned the settlement of Massachusetts Bay which was the source of all the other colonies of New England.

Virginia was in a dying state and seemed to revive and flourish from the example of New England.

Several modern historians have pointed out that the Founding Fathers regarded "pursuit of happiness", not as an individual chase after titillation and pleasure, but as a practical cultivation of material well being, survival and spiritual uplift. The emphasis is on "spiritual uplift".

The classical view, exemplified in the "Pilgrim ethic" and handed down through intervening generations, was that happiness is not a goal in itself but a by-product of religious faith, devotion to high personal standards, helpfulness to others and productive work. In short, happiness is not a "situation we arrive at but a method of traveling".

For generations Americans have shared certitudes of faith in God, national destiny and the ultimate rewards of virtue in their life and in the hereafter. They accepted the basic values of personal integrity. They found the family group to be stabilizing. They held to the anchor of closely knit community.

The Pilgrims knew the essential ingredients of human progress and happiness to be spiritual satisfaction and moral excellence.

Every tree needs roots to thrive. Society without roots in the fundamental doctrine of devotion and duty will wither and die. Chaos and unhappiness and empty lives are the fruits of a "do as you please" philosophy.

By the same token, no man is truly happy who does not make his contribution to the society in which he lives. The highest satisfaction results from performance within his ability.

A review of our past, a study of our progress, a knowledge of the sacrifice and devotion that produced our present material well-being and our security may prove instructive to those who are impelled to take a cynical approach to our present-day problems. An awareness on our part that we are not alone, or even the originators of the "searching experience", makes it possible to face the future with greater confidence and with infinitely better attitudes and methods.

The Pilgrims have been described as the "dissenters" of their day. And so they were, in the best meaning of the word. They reacted to a "Merry Old England" that was a combination of moral permissiveness, political brutality and stringent state-church discipline.

They reached for concepts that were beyond their time and comprehension. They have been ridiculed for their alleged rigidity. But a less determined people could not have succeeded under the conditions then existing.

Further, much of this criticism, as we have seen, is the result of confusion and ignorance—especially a persistent confusion of the Pilgrims with the Puritans.

In the Pilgrim story, several significant themes stand out:

1. They were tolerant in a day of vast intolerance.

2. They conceived and staked their lives and fortunes on the principles of religious freedom.

3. They enunciated the principle of control of the church by the people, not by the sovereign. In time, this came to be restated as the separation of the church and state.

4. They adopted the Mayflower Compact, the first promulgation of the principle of government by the consent of the governed on this continent.

5. They established the concept that was to evolve into the New England Town Meeting, in which each citizen could have a voice, where varying opinions could be constructively compromised and where each citizen accepted responsibilities for the welfare of all.

6. They perfected a system of individual ownership of property, in contrast to the old English system of place and privilege, including control of land.

7. They established the system of American justice founded on the grand jury system and the right of every man to a jury trial.

These make up a list that is especially impressive in the face of the meager numbers in the Pilgrim colony. One does not seek to give them all the credit for these contributions to, and enrichment of, American life. But they did plant the seeds, and nurture them.

Other colonies had been founded to exploit the new land. They were not marked initially by singular success. By contrast, the Pilgrims came to build homes and a new society. They came not to despoil or destroy but to fulfill a destiny that was greater than they knew. They set an example that was to be emulated by the other colonies. They espoused principles that were to be borrowed and to survive in our American institutions.

There was much more than dissent in all of this. There was the unifying influence of their faith—a strong religious motivation. Out of this and a fixed constructive impulse was born a purpose that became known ultimately as the American "pioneering spirit".

And so the Pilgrims' dream, based on their faith in God and the eternal rightness of things, became the American dream. They built their lives on it, they exemplified it. They, and those who were to follow, knew who they were and what they had to do. They knew reality and they faced it, even through bitter hardship. And the nation prospered.

When Alexis de Tocqueville, the French political philosopher, published his celebrated study of American social and political institutions in 1832 he recorded a salient finding:

> *America is great because America is good; and if America ever ceases to be good, America will cease to be great.*

During the turmoil of the late 1960s and early 1970s there were many who wondered if that time had come. Our nation seemed to lose its guiding purpose, to falter. The period was marked by a crisis of confidence in our leadership at all levels, a crisis of confidence in our ideals and, in truth, a crisis of confidence in ourselves.

Norman Cousins, then editor of the *Saturday Review*, echoing Tocqueville, wisely observed, "America will become great again when we re-examine the things that made us great in the first place."

And, happily, the great spiritual and moral reserves built up over the years have helped the nation to alter course and take the road back. We have come a long way.

The 1980s have been named the "Re Decade". We have regenerated our optimism, recaptured our unity and restored our purpose. This retrospective is intended to guide the rediscovery process and to inspire our future morale, aspirations, and resolve.

The author of these commentaries voiced many of these thoughts in Plymouth at the Triennial Congress of the Mayflower Society in his keynote address September 11, 1978. Concluding this final chapter of *Stepping Stones*, we quote from those remarks:

> *Sociologist Danial Bell has said that societies do not hang together unless they have a strong core of religion—not in a formalized sectarian way but in the broad sense of moral discipline and human character—principles such as pervade all the great religions.*

> *This means that there is a moral authority that underlies modern civilization and, if you destroy or neglect it, you put at risk an orderly society and invite chaos.*

> *The men and women gathered here today have a charge to keep. Patrick Henry reminded his country men that a free people to*

remain free must continuously re-examine itself. 'I know of no way of judging the future,' he said, 'but by the past.' 'Liberty,' he added, 'is rooted in order.'

But, there is a special message for this group of Mayflower descendents in an excerpt from a talk by an unheralded speaker at the laying of the cornerstone for the National Monument to the Forefathers August 2, 1859, just a few blocks from the site where we now meet.

This heroic statue of faith, emblazoning the principles of morality, law, education and liberty, was undertaken by a Pilgrim Society that numbered only 3412 members. The Civil War, and the colossal costs involved, delayed its completion until 1889.

But on that day at the cornerstone laying some of the nation's outstanding orators, including Richard Warren, W. M. Evarts, Salmon P. Chase, and John P. Hale, expounded on the virtues of the enterprise with flaming rhetoric.

The actual laying of the stone was supervised by the grand master of the Grand Masonic Lodge of Massachusetts, Col. John T. Heard. His remarks were epitomized in one discerning and moving sentence:

'A People capable of greatness will not forget the virtues of their fathers; reverently will they cherish them and gratefully present them in all their luster for the respect and imitiation of after ages.'

Because of our heritage, because of our strong sense of history we are entrusted with the privilege of fostering the study of American Beginnings—at Plymouth and elsewhere throughout the nation.

'America will become great again when we re-examine the things that made us great in the first place.'

The Plymouth Founders knew and passed the lesson to us who would follow in their footsteps that rights cannot be demanded without acceptance of responsibilities that are their counterparts. Only then can we be truly free. This is the legacy of the Pilgrims.

The time is propitious for America to look back and find its soul.

*yea, though they should be but even as **stepping stones** unto others for the performance of so great a work.*

William Bradford.
Of Plymouth Plantation

The End

EDITING COMMITTEE: Benjamin Franklin, John Adams and Thomas Jefferson editing Jefferson's draft of the Declaration of Independence. An adaptation by the late Ernest Richardson from painting by J.L.G. Ferris which hangs in Independence Hall, Philadelphia.

Bibliography

Our bibliography was derived from four libraries besides our own: Boston Public Library, Library of Congress, New York Public Library and Portland, Oregon's Multnomah County Library. We list the volumes we have studied.

Primary Sources

Bradford, William. *Of Plymouth Plantation*. Commonwealth of Massachusetts Edition. Boston: Wright and Porter, 1898.

Bradford, William. *Of Plymouth Plantation: 1606 - 1646*. Edited by W. T. Davis. New York: Charles Scribner and Sons, 1908.

Bradford, William. *Of Plymouth Plantation: 1620 - 1647*. Edited by Samuel E. Morison. New York: Alfred A.Knopf, 1952.

Cheever, George B. *Journal of the Pilgrims*. New York and London: John Wiley, 1848.

Dexter, Henry Martyn. *Mourt's Relation*. Boston: J.K. Wiggin, 1865.

Young, Alexander. *Chronicles of the Pilgrim Fathers*. Boston: Little-Brown, 1841.

Secondary Sources

Arber, Edward. *Story of the Pilgrim Fathers*. Boston and New York: Houghton Mifflin, 1897.

Belknap, Jeremy. *American Biography*. Boston: Thomas and Andrew, 1794.

Cushman, Robert. *The Sin and Danger of Self Love*. First sermon preached in New England, 1621; England, 1622.

Morton, Nathaniel. *New England's Memorial*. Cambridge, 1669.

Pory, John. *Lost Description of Plymouth Colony*. Burrage-Brown University Library Treasure, 1918.

Winslow, Edward. *Good News from New England*. Massachusetts Historical Society Collection, Series I, Volume 8, 1624.

Illustrated Pilgrim Memorial. Boston: printed by R. M. Edwards, 1863.

Other Sources

Archer, Gleason. *Mayflower Heroes*. New York: Appleton-Century Co., 1935.

Bartlett, Robert M. *The Pilgrim Way*. Philadelphia: Pilgrim Press, 1971.

Bartlett, William Henry, and Hall, A. *Pilgrim Fathers or Founders of New England*. London: Virtue and Co.

Boorstin, Daniel J., ed. *An American Primer*. Chicago: University of Chicago Press, 1966.

Bowen, Catherine Drinker. *John Adams and the American Revolution*. Boston: Little, Brown and Co., 1950.

Craven, Wesley Frank. *Legend of the Founding Fathers*. New York: New York University Press, 1956.

Goodwin, John A. *Pilgrim Republic*. Boston: Houghton-Mifflin Co., 1920.

Gregg, Frank Moody. *Story of the Pilgrim Fathers*. Cleveland: A.H. Clark Co., 1915.

Hale, William Harlan. *The March of Freedom*. New York and London: Harper & Brothers, 1947.

Hanks, Charles Stedman. *Our Plymouth Forefathers, the real founders of our Republic*. Boston: Davis Estes and Co., 1907.

Lord, Arthur. *Plymouth and the Pilgrims*. Boston: Houghton-Mifflin Co., 1920.

Masefield, John. *Chronicle of the Pilgrim Fathers*, 1910.

Morison, S. E. *The American Revolution and the Federal Constitution*. New York: Oxford University Press, 1956.

Peterson, Merrill D. *Thomas Jefferson and the New Nation*. New York: Oxford University Press, 1970.

Smith, Bradford. *Bradford of Plymouth*. Boston and New York: J. B. Lippencott Co., 1951.

Talbot, Archie Lee. *John Carver*. Library of Congress, 1927.

Usher, Roland Greene. *The Pilgrims and their History*. McMillan Co., 1920.

Index

chosen governor of *Mayflower*, 28; confirmed governor of Colony at Cape Cod, 36; friendly contact with Massasoit, Treaty of Peace, 73-74; died of sunstroke, 78; considered to have written *Mourt's Relation*, 164-170

Cattle, first: (1624) 103

Charlestown: Massachusetts Bay Colony organizes with Governor John Winthrop, 132-34

Civil Government: John Robinson's advice, "Choose to govern those who entirely love and will promote the common good," 26

Communism: Pilgrims resisted, end of common course, 97; land apportionment by families, 97-98, 140-42

Constitution, U.S., 171-84; 186-90

Corn, Indian: explorers found Indian baskets with corn and filled ship's kettle, 49; intention to pay natives, 50-51; corn planted with fish, 78; more precious than silver, 103

Corn Hill: place where corn was found north of Little Pamet River, 52

Cotton, Rev. John: admonishes Puritans, 133

Cushman, Robert: assistant to John Carver as negotiator with Virginia Company, 13-15; later with Adventurers in London, 17-20; reproved by Pastor Robinson, 21; did not sail on *Mayflower*, 31; arrived on *Fortune* November, 1621; stayed two weeks, preached "first sermon", 81; brought charter to sign, 82; took *Journal of the Pilgrims* with him for publication, 84

Deane, Charles: Acquired long hand transcript of lost Bradford manuscript, xxii

Debt, 114, 120, 136

Declaration of Independence, 171-84

Defense measures: fort built, 91; town impaled, 85

De Rasieres, Isaak: Secretary of New Netherland, visited Plymouth in 1627 and gave good appraisal of Pilgrims, 121, 148

De Tocqueville, Alex, 196

Dutch: relations at Leyden, 191

Emerson, Ralph Waldo, 163

Endecott, Governor John: established settlement in Salem in 1628, brought Leyden passengers, 132; wrote for help from Dr. Fuller in curing sick, 126-27

Fish, 80, 98, 100

Franklin, Dr. Benjamin, 178, 183

Fortune: arrived late November, 1621, with 35 colonists, 81

Fulham Palace Library: Bradford manuscript found there, xxii

Fuller, Dr. Samuel: sent by Bradford to Salem to give aid to sick, 126-27

General or Generality: former course dissolved, 110; share and share alike with Planters and Adventurers, 18-19

Good News from New England, 157

Heard, Col. John T.: spoke at laying of cornerstone for National Monument at Plymouth, 135, 197

Henry, Patrick: on liberty, 196-97